Intention

MIKE JAMES ROSS   SEKOUL THEODOR KRASTEV   DAN PILAT

Intention

The Surprising Psychology
of High Performers

WILEY

Published by John Wiley & Sons, Inc., Hoboken, New Jersey.
Published simultaneously in Canada.

For general information on our other products and services or for technical support, please contact our Customer Care Department within the United States at (800) 762-2974, outside the United States at (317) 572-3993 or fax (317) 572-4002.

Wiley also publishes its books in a variety of electronic formats. Some content that appears in print may not be available in electronic formats. For more information about Wiley products, visit our web site at www.wiley.com.

Library of Congress Cataloging-in-Publication Data:

ISBN 9781394189151 (Cloth)
ISBN 9781394189168 (ePub)
ISBN 9781394189175 (ePDF)

Cover Design and Image: © Laurence Anton
Author Photos: Courtesy of the Authors
Printed and bound by CPI Group (UK) Ltd, Croydon, CR0 4YY

C9781394189151_250124

To our families, friends, and colleagues. Thank you.

Contents

PART I

Fundamentals

CHAPTER 1

Introduction

"Do not go where the path may lead, go instead where there is no path and leave a trail."

—Ralph Waldo Emerson

Why Intention?

We're stuck. Stuck to the couch. Stuck scrolling. Stuck at work. Stuck in worn-out paths of habitual action. Stuck in patterns and echo chambers of thought. Stuck in carefully curated lives where we've traded our agency for endless comforts that wrap us in existential ennui.

As our eyes fixate on a constant parade of images meant to engage us, we notice something in the periphery. We see folks who are just like us, except they seem to be deeply happy and fulfilled. They go through life with ease and grace, overcoming obstacles and making amazing things happen for themselves.

Peering closer, we see that they aren't gods or superhumans. They're just people who have chosen to not be stuck and decided to become the "main characters" in their own lives. Their success (as they define it!) is not a birthright bestowed upon a lucky few, but the result of lives lived with intention.

Take a moment right now to imagine a different version of yourself. A superhero in your daily life. Your superpower? Infinite self-control. Your circumstances haven't changed one bit, but you suddenly have the power to deeply engage with everything you do and unstick yourself. Visualize this and think about your life. What would you do differently in your day-to-day life (e.g., how would your morning routine change)? What would your life look and feel like? How would this new way of being affect your feelings about yourself? What about the value you bring to your family, friends, and colleagues?

This exercise is more than a fantasy—it's a challenge. One that we spend the rest of this book preparing you to face.

Borrowing from a wide variety of related disciplines—philosophy, psychology, religion, neuroscience, and organizational management to name a few—we focus on the five key ingredients of intention: willpower, curiosity, integrity, attention, and habits. For each ingredient, we provide an overview of the current scientific understanding of why they are important and how they work. More importantly, we provide information that's actionable, and present you with knowledge and methods that you can actually apply to your working and personal life to gain a higher sense of agency, authenticity, and engagement in everything you do. Intention is an expression of our identity, and to live without it is to lose ourselves. Our aim is to help you reconnect with that power in you.

No, These Traits Are Not Innate and Immutable

Some combination of willpower, curiosity, integrity, attention, and habits can be found in every high performer and recent research shows that they're strong predictors of success. But there's a second reason why we focus on these, which speaks more broadly to how we can claim our agency and lead fuller lives: The other thing these five ingredients have in common is that many of us were taught (and still believe—see the following survey data) that they're innate, and we're born with a fixed amount of each. They are not. And in this book we show, with scientific evidence, that each of them is highly trainable, and we teach you how to train them. If there's any aspect of your life you want to excel in, whether work, home, sports, the arts, or spirituality, you can exercise these five aspects of intention and improve.

Nearly 50% of people believe that willpower, curiosity, integrity, attention, and habit formation are inherent traits that cannot be trained.[1]

Although this book is based around the science behind each of these aspects, as with any story told with science, this is not the full picture—which is why we also illustrate our points with case studies, stories, diagrams, and drawings that support the idea that no matter who you are or how you approach these ingredients, you can use them to become more intentional.

Our core message is that intention can be trained—not just a fleeting feeling of agency, but the real application of intention that improves our lives and the lives of those around us.

What Do We Mean by *High Performance?*

This book focuses on the skills of high performers—not their ability to run consecutive marathons or lead Fortune 500 teams, but their willpower, curiosity, integrity, attention, and habits. We understand and love that high performers don't always have traditionally lofty achievements to their name—maybe they only ran one marathon, or maybe they took a walk around the block for the first time in decades. We see high performance not as a competition against others or the attaining of some objective standard, but as a way of life. What sets our high performers apart from the rest of us is their ability to act with intention. These aren't just CEOs and top athletes; they're students, stay-at-home parents, minimum-wage workers, and artists. Despite the limits of their circumstances, these individuals harness the power of intention and—in some cases—are able to radiate that feeling of intention to others.

Consequently, for us, high performance can be domain-specific (eating 25 hotdogs in 10 minutes) or not (being a generally "good" person). It can be outwardly reflected (Michael Phelps's long list of wins) or something much more personal (a 67-year-old getting over their life-long fear of driving). It can lead to "Success" (big *S*, as defined by society) or "success" (small *s*, as defined by how you see a life well lived).

We're not passing judgment or comparing the ways each of us can exhibit high performance. We define *high performance* as: "the ability to do subjectively hard things." So if your goal is to eat a lot of hot dogs quickly, more power to you—we'll help you get there as best we can. We are also there for you if your vision of high performance is about making the world better. On that front, there has never been a time that doing hard things has been needed more, and we can all increase our impact by strengthening the five skills in this book. Intention is not a cure-all for languishing and disengagement. In some cases these feelings might have deeper roots than we're qualified to address. But we've found that being more intentional in our lives has helped us to break out of moments of languish and get unstuck.

Beyond the Individual

This book is an answer to the corporate challenge of improving engagement at work. By building intentional teams using the five core muscle groups of intention, you can improve how your colleagues are performing and give them back a sense of autonomy. In doing so, we can together create more dynamic, adaptable, and resilient organizations. Additionally, by addressing the challenge of languishing and applying intention in one aspect of your life, you can dramatically improve how you exercise intention in all other aspects. Becoming more intentional in your own life is good for your family, your community, and for society at large. This is not only because your level of engagement will be contagious to those around you, but also because you will be contributing your best to the world—at whatever scale and in whatever areas you choose.

About Us

While much of this story revolves around what it means to be a high performer and how to get there, we're not claiming to always fit the bill ourselves. We're certainly working hard at it, but we're on a journey just like everyone else. That said, we do know a lot about applied behavioral science and how to motivate people. Bringing that knowledge to you is what this book is all about.

Dan and *Sekoul* are co-founders of The Decision Lab (TDL), an applied research and innovation firm that uses behavioral science to generate social impact. They were roommates in Toronto, where Dan worked in banking and Sekoul was a consultant at the Boston Consulting Group. They decided to take their backgrounds (in decision systems and neuroscience) to build an organization that would be intentional about the type of work it does. TDL works with some of the largest organizations in the world, carrying out research in priority areas and running one of the most popular publications in applied behavioral science. In the past, they've helped organizations such as the Bill & Melinda Gates Foundation, Capital One, the World Bank, and many Fortune 500s solve some of their thorniest problems using scientific thinking.

Mike is a former lawyer, private equity investor, McKinsey consultant, and startup founder who is currently the CHRO for a large Canadian retailer, helping motivate and engage more than 5,000 employees while maintaining a unique corporate culture that has lasted for more than 180 years. For him, his highest performance is raising his children to be good citizens and intentional in their own right.

CHAPTER 2

A Languishing World

"I would prefer not to."
— Herman Melville, *Bartleby, the Scrivener*

There's a powerful gravity to modern life, pulling us toward routine, passivity, and meaningless actions. We've all been victims of this force. It lures us to the couch when we should go for a run. It tempts us to watch TV instead of starting that creative project. It hinders us from taking a chance on love, taking control of our lives, and living up to our true potential.

In short, a staple of modern life is being in a state of languish. Neither mentally healthy nor mentally ill, just in a generalized "blahness." Coined by Corey Keyes in the early 2000s, *languish* is an emptiness and stagnation, constituting "a life of quiet despair." People who languish describe themselves and their lives as "hollow," "empty," "a shell," and "a void."[1] As eloquently expressed by Adam Grant in his widely read *New York Times* piece, languishing comes with "the dulling of delight and the dwindling of drive."[2]

How did we get here? How is it possible that in an era that has blessed us with longer life expectancy, and in societies with unprecedented comfort and security, we find ourselves grappling with escalating depression,[3] anxiety,[4] and suicide rates?[5] Why is it that the same modern technology and tools that have made us almost godlike compared to our ancestors leave many of us feeling powerless?

How is it that workplaces, that have never cared so much about fostering purpose and meaning, feel meaningless and empty? And why is it that more people than ever express a sense of disengagement or loss of interest and motivation?

The root of this disengagement is tremendously complex.[6] One reason is that many of us live in an era of ease and convenience, where everything is taken care of. And in our work, we strive for higher and higher levels of specialization. So we can be more efficient. So we can be more successful. But while we were busy delegating the mundane to gain that success, we also delegated our agency along with it. We've created a world where each of us has limitless options and no real choices, and our answer to that is to disengage and stop fully participating in our lives.

As Far as the Eye Can See

Now for the good news: languishing and disengagement aren't necessarily signs of personal failure. They're often consequences of our environment. Think of the last time you felt that you weren't where you should be, and instead of making the effort to change your circumstance, you felt there was no hope. When we languish, we feel a combination of "I need to get out of here" and "meh, not likely," and too often we then opt not to act.

While it's tempting to blame the rise of the internet and our increasing lack of community, languishing isn't entirely new. In the late 1800s, Émile Durkheim used *anomie* to describe the sense of disconnection that modern production lines created in industrial laborers. Even Plato identified a similar feeling in *akrasia*: a strong sense of "I should," followed by acting against our better judgment and not doing anything.

Languishing isn't limited to North American society either—take Japan's *hikikomori* movement. The country's economic stagnation in the 1990s, combined with social pressure and mental health challenges, resulted in a modern-day hermit movement. Up to a million Japanese citizens live as recluses, remaining at home while avoiding work and personal connections. *Hikikomori* is even thought to be growing, not just in Japan, but globally.[7]

Languishing and Self-Destruction

In response to our loss of agency, we find ways to take control of our lives. But our usual responses tend to cause more harm than help. There are extremes, like the abuse of alcohol or drugs, but also small day-to-day behaviors: bingeing meaningless television shows, neglecting our physical health, eating too much sugar, or failing to make time for quality connections.

Why do we turn to self-destructive choices? Edgar Allen Poe explained our tendency to procrastinate when we know we shouldn't, calling this *The Imp of the Perverse*:

> We have a task before us which must be speedily performed. We know that it will be ruinous to make delay. The most important crisis of our life calls, trumpet-tongued, for immediate energy and action. We glow, we are consumed with eagerness to commence the work, with the anticipation of whose glorious result our whole souls are on fire. It must, it shall be undertaken to-day, and yet we put it off until to-morrow, and why?[8]

Our self-destructive choices are evidence of how our deep-seated drive for agency manifests itself wherever it can. Sometimes it feels like the only decisions we get to make are bad ones. Take the modern phenomenon of *bàofùxìng áoyè*, or as it's translated from Chinese, "revenge bedtime procrastination." Journalist Daphne K. Lee used the term to describe what happens when individuals "who don't have much control over their daytime life refuse to sleep early in order to regain some sense of freedom during late-night hours."[9] If you've ever done something that you know is bad for you just to feel free, you'll understand this.

Suggestions for overcoming bad bedtime habits generally come in the form of establishing rules for better sleep discipline, like avoiding technology before bed. But revenge bedtime procrastinators know the tips and tricks for better sleep and still choose to stay up. As one bedtime procrastinator put it, "It's a way of revolting against all the obligations that you have. Because, well, my life, and I think the life of most adults, consists of lots and lots of obligations."[10]

These procrastinators are simply reclaiming freedom via one of the only outlets they have. We don't need a reminder to put down our phone before bedtime. We need space to make choices for ourselves. We need to exercise the basic human need to decide our own destiny. If you relate to the bedtime procrastinator—perhaps to a lesser extreme or in another domain—you're not alone. In our survey, 63% of people agreed they sometimes do things that are bad for them just to feel like they're in control. So, the next time you find yourself scrolling rather than sleeping, realize that part of the reason you're doing so is that you want to feel free to choose (and that maybe there's a healthier way to feel that).

> 63% of people say they do things that they know are self-destructive to feel a sense of control.

The Decline of Workplace Autonomy

Perhaps nowhere is more prone to languishing than the workplace. It's no coincidence that Émile Durkheim's *anomie* came at the advent of the industrial revolution. Unless work is designed to combat it, languishing will persist. Case in point, a whopping 77% of workers around the world were disengaged at work in 2022.[11]

And despite employers' best efforts, workplace disengagement has been increasing for quite some time. The rise of efficiency tools has dramatically reduced autonomy for workers. Managers are given clear scripts for what they can and cannot say to their teams; directors have defined measurement tools like Objectives and Key Results (OKRs) and Key Performance Indicators (KPIs) to meet on a daily, weekly, monthly, quarterly, and annual basis. No one gets to decide for themselves anymore.

Languishing in our personal lives and feeling disengaged at work come from the same root: lack of freedom and satisfaction. Unfortunately, most pieces of advice on engagement given to managers are, as with our personal lives, aimed at the wrong aspect of the problem. Rather than giving workers more autonomy and a sense of control, we try to fix disengagement by building mission statements or communicating purpose—emphasizing the meaningfulness of the work. Purpose statements are important, but they're not enough. We need agency, and with it, identity, first. Without agency, meaning and purpose have nowhere to root.

Unfortunately, individual autonomy is often viewed as a distraction from more important goals like consistency, efficiency, and productivity, and as such, it is seen as dangerous and unproductive.

Ironically, not only does a lack of autonomy cause disengagement, but organizational outcomes also suffer. Events like the COVID pandemic exposed the vulnerability that anchoring on hyper-efficiency and leanness causes in modern workplaces. When unanticipated events occurred, the companies leading in modern management science were the ones left high and dry. By decreasing autonomy, we've decreased organizations' ability to respond to change and disruption.

Every single one of us has the power to overcome disengagement and reclaim intentionality. However, the forces against us get stronger all the time. These forces express themselves in a myriad of ways, from the proliferation of social media, to pressure from our families,

co-workers, and peers. At work, these manifest in the reduction of real choices and the separation of our working selves from our true nature. The effort to resist these forces is getting harder as the distractions and tools of sabotage get stronger, but that doesn't mean that we have to let them rule our lives and stop us from realizing our potential as human beings.

CHAPTER 3

What Is Intention?

"When spiders unite they can tie down a lion"
　　　　　　　　　　　　　　　　　　　—Ethiopian Proverb

When humans first appeared on Earth 300,000 years ago, *Homo sapiens* were hardly the only hominid around. We likely shared the planet with five to seven other hominid species. Some of them, such as the Neanderthals, were likely bigger and stronger than we were, and as far as we can tell from their skulls, they also had significantly bigger brains. While modern humans have a cranial capacity of about 82 cubic inches (1,344 cubic cm), Neanderthals could reach up to 100. Brain size accounts for only 9–16% of overall variability in intelligence, but nevertheless, Neanderthals had an advantage over us.[1] Despite their physical advantages, these hominids died out 40,000 years ago. But "died out" is perhaps not the right terminology here—they thrived for a long time until we came to Europe and "outcompeted" them (sometimes by eating their food, other times by murder).[2]

What did we have that our brethren didn't? The answer likely lies in how we used our brains rather than our brawn. While factors such as our access to fire certainly helped, perhaps the most important difference between us and other hominids was our ability to use social cooperation, complex language, and abstract concepts. Our ability to plan, communicate, and work together allowed us to overcome our physical limitations, especially in groups. Our special brains allowed us to transcend the here and now, formulate complex beliefs, share them with others, and to work together.

Rather than focusing exclusively on our immediate survival needs, we could *mentally time-travel*. We could formulate complex plans that anticipated, and more importantly, created an unseen future. What set us apart wasn't our physique, or even tools like fire, but something invisible: our shared intention.[3]

Intention as a Survival Tool

Various fields such as anthropology, evolutionary biology, and developmental psychology have spent decades studying how shared intention evolved, how it helped us outcompete other species, and how it manifests in people today. Some of the most impactful work on this comes from Michael Tomasello, a developmental psychologist based at Duke University. In research spanning decades, Tomasello has argued that social cognition is the "secret sauce" of being human. He points out that nonhuman primates are unable to do many tasks that come easily to humans: over-imitating (copying the style of an action, not just the action itself), recursive mind reading (being aware of what another person knows we know), and social learning through deliberate transmission (intentionally teaching each other how to interact with others).

While it's hard to say exactly how we evolved to have these abilities, they likely developed as a result of environmental pressures. Around 2 million years ago, and again 200,000 years ago, resources were scarce—but not so bad that everyone died off. This resulted in a Goldilocks situation that allowed only certain types of individuals to survive: those who learned to collaborate. Too much adversity, and the group of early hominids would die off. Too little adversity, and they wouldn't be exposed to enough selective pressures to force evolution toward any particular trait. However, with just the right level of adversity and enough time, these pressures can knock down walls between individuals, forcing them to share thoughts, ideas, and intentions. If this happens in an isolated situation, individuals might put their heads together, come up with a solution, and go on with their lives. But when the environment itself rewards shared goals, over generations, the result is a species that has advantages beyond the ability to coordinate together in the present moment.

What Are *Shared Intentions*?

While coordinated intentions and shared intentions may look somewhat similar, shared intentions are more than mere coordination. To illustrate this point, one of the most famous philosophers of the last hundred years, John Searle, created a thought experiment.[4] Imagine two groups of people: picnickers eating in a park, and a dance troupe practicing for a recital. Picture the following scenarios:

- A rainstorm breaks out, and the picnickers run for cover under the trees.
- The dance troupe practices a routine in which they run for cover under the trees.

What's the difference between these two scenarios? According to Searle, it's the difference between what he calls *I-intentions* and *We-intentions*. While the coordinated action of the picnickers looks like shared intention, it's actually a group of individuals acting in self-interest. Their actions happen to coincide because they're responding to the same stimuli, so they express self-interest in a way that may appear coordinated. The dance troupe, on the other hand, has deliberately chosen to collaborate and coordinate. They show We-intentions. The same may be true for other animals, which coordinate actions that seem to express shared intention, but in most cases, they demonstrably act in coordinated self-interest.[5]

This brings us to an important point, which runs throughout the book: the same behavior (including what some may deem "high performance") can be connected to different internal mechanisms. This is less obvious when observing a group of people running in the park. But it becomes extremely obvious when you consider some of the incredible results of human intention throughout history.

Intention, Passed on as a Flame

To accomplish complex goals that are distant in the future, we must persevere. This ability to continue working towards a goal is the crux of what we think of as intention (as opposed to deciding to pick up a pencil). But it's far from our limit. As we've seen throughout history, intention can far outlive an individual. When Qin Shi Huang became the First Emperor of the Qin dynasty in 221 BCE, one of his most important projects was to unify a set of walls that he and his opponents had built in what is now China. That set of defenses, which originally began between the 8th and 5th centuries BCE, evolved, expanded, and continued until well into the 16th century. They resulted in what is commonly known as the Great Wall of China, one of the largest human-made structures with 10,051 wall sections, 1,764 ramparts or trenches, 29,510 individual buildings, and 2,211 fortifications or passes, stretching a total length of 13,170.70 miles (21,196.18 km).

When he started, did Qin Shi Huang imagine that his wall would repel foreign invaders for multiple millennia? Or attract over 10 million tourists per year in the distant 21st century? Probably not. Whatever his initial vision was, his will became a collective will. Hundreds of thousands of workers over thousands of years lived in service of that wall (admittedly, they probably didn't all share the same intention, but enough people did for the project to continue). The idea that the wall must exist spread like wildfire, carrying his vision from one generation to the next. That's the power of shared intention.

From an individualistic point of view, it seems unnatural that we should care about a distant future we'll never live to see. But it's this level of intentional action—stretching out across people, places, and centuries—that makes *Homo sapiens* unique.

Intention and Self in the Modern Age

As the world has evolved, we have willed ever-more complicated things into existence. Putting a person on the moon is hard. Beyond the immediate technological challenges, think of the sustained human effort that was put into developing those technologies. Each generation picked up the mantle from the previous one. First, we were generalists, focused on the nature of the universe. Then, we started to branch off, with specialists in math, chemistry, and physics. As the technologies became more complex, we began to specialize even further, with thought leaders spending entire lifetimes on a single formula. Only after countless lifetimes spent solving a series of tiny problems did we finally get to the last small step. That step was a great accomplishment, but it was also an inevitable expression of our identity as humans and a great leap for us all.

And intention is, above all, an expression of identity. Our sense of self—in an individual it might be called consciousness, ego, or a soul, whereas in a group it might be an allegiance or loyalty—is a vehicle that transports intention through time. Intention has proven to be one of the most powerful tools we have.

We have the power to will our goals and ideas into existence. But without the right approach, we might spend our entire lives manifesting an identity that isn't truly our own. Our book is based on the idea that the sense of languishing or disengagement that so many people feel today is the result of exactly that—carrying out a will that is not our own. In the following chapters, therefore, we explore what science has to say about intention and how we might apply those concepts to become more authentic and critical humans.

CHAPTER 4

Becoming Main Characters

"Most people are other people. Their thoughts are someone else's opinions, their lives a mimicry, their passions a quotation."

—Oscar Wilde

In the 2021 movie *Free Guy*, Ryan Reynolds is an NPC—a non-playable character—in a video game. One day, he becomes self-aware, shown by him making the ultimate self-affirming choice: asking for a cappuccino instead of drip coffee.

Seeing the stunned looks of the barista and the other clients in the cafe, he quickly goes back to his regular order, but the damage has been done. He has, in a moment of awakening, realized that he doesn't need to follow the script. He has free will. He can choose what to do. As he asks for his cappuccino, Ryan Reynolds starts to become a Main Character, able to make decisions. As he leaves the coffee shop, we see a confused awakening on the face of the barista, who is maybe discovering that freedom is also possible for her.

But there is much more to this event in the movie's plot development than meets the eye. Reynolds' insight isn't only that he doesn't have to follow the script, it's that he *has* been following a script. When we make choices, we usually believe that we're deciding for ourselves. It can be jarring to acknowledge how strongly we're influenced by others, whether it be parents, social media, or marketing.

If asked whether we'd like to live as NPCs or Main Characters, most of us would claim to prefer building our own destinies. This makes sense. Research by Roy Baumeister and Lauren Brewer has shown that just believing in free will is positively correlated with life satisfaction, finding life meaningful, lower levels of stress, self-efficacy, and self-control.[1] Who wouldn't want to be *Free Guy*?

The problem? Freedom is much harder than it sounds. First, we live in societies with other people, and as a consequence, we're constrained by shared intentions. While shared intentions have allowed us to progress far beyond our primate cousins, they often come at the sacrifice of personal choice. Navigating these waters successfully is a significant part of what defines a Main Character.

We may have evolved the ability to collectively act on ideas and build things like the Great Wall of China. But at a personal level, that shared intention often comes at the cost of individuation, pushing us to follow goals that were never our own to begin with. A C-suite executive might spend her career chasing status and money, only to realize she never really wanted them in the first place but was just adopting society's idea of a good life. A son or daughter who makes big life decisions to please demanding parents might realize that he or she is not satisfied with these accomplishments. It's not that these folks aren't acting with intention. They've learned to act on someone else's intention. The cost of this misplaced identification can be enormous—both for the individual and for society.

We must also acknowledge that it's a lot easier for some to exercise freedom than others. Many are limited in their choices due to various circumstances, such as differences in gender, sexuality, race, ability, or socioeconomics, and so on. However, it's equally true that there's always an opportunity to express some choice. As Viktor Frankl said, "Everything can be taken from a man but one thing: the last of the human freedoms—to choose one's attitude in any given set of circumstances, to choose one's own way."[2] So how do we go about making those choices like the Main Characters we want to be?

Intentionality 101: Making Choices

As the ancient Greek philosopher Heraclitus maintained, life is a constant state of change. This means that we need to focus on the process rather than the destination, and concentrate on making the choices that are available to us, no matter how small they are. Life isn't about deciding to order a cappuccino instead of a coffee, but the goal is to become more cognizant of the scripts we are following and make the choices we can. These small choices add up, and also help prepare us for bigger ones in the future.

These might even begin with choosing to copy others. We all know folks who can inspire us to become Main Characters. No matter where or how you live, you've met people who embody this mindset. They're not necessarily the richest or the fanciest, but they're the ones you want to spend time with. They make you feel inspired just by being around them because they are living their own, full lives that haven't been predetermined for them.

There's nothing external limiting your ability to be more like these people. You don't need anything other than the intention to make it happen. But the simplicity of the path to become a Main Character doesn't make it an easy one. Becoming a Main Character is the work of a lifetime, but that work can start at any time and in any place. Fortunately, there are plenty of people to serve as inspiration—from history as well as in our daily lives. And just like the barista in *Free Guy*, these inspiring figures push us to be more ourselves, not more like them.

At a global training program in Singapore, Mike (one of the authors of this book) met a very successful, 22-year-old Japanese consultant who told him: "I was at the top of my class in elementary school, top of my class at a very competitive high school, and then graduated at the top of my class from the best university in my country." Then, after a long pause, he asked, "How can I figure out what it is that I want to do with my life?" He had all the trappings of success you could wish for but wasn't really living. He was living the life that his parents, his society, and now his superiors wanted him to live. Most distressing was that he had been living for others so fully and completely that he had lost touch with what he really wanted.

He was living someone else's dreams, acting as an NPC. Meeting Mike, who at that point had shifted away from the traditional consulting achievement path, unlocked in him a question: how can I be who I want to be, not who others' want me to be?

It's easy to trick ourselves into thinking traditional success is an indication of being a Main Character. But when we really ask ourselves why we do what we do, we invariably see how much of our behavior is a result of other people's perceptions. So many of our decisions are dictated by the expectations of others.

As a short exercise, take a few minutes and ask yourself this: how much of what you do, even of who you are, comes from real choices that you made for yourself, as opposed to from following the advice and wishes of your parents, your friends, your bosses, and so on? This is not necessarily about "doing what you love," with all of the complexities that trying to find that elusive thing can bring. It is about doing what you decided to do, rather than just going along with a set of choices that others have made for you.

As is discussed in Chapter 3, we may be shocked to discover that we are following someone else's script or that we have created an identity that we don't identify with. We may also discover that we don't even know how to begin creating our own.

As a consequence of societal and family pressures, we are all subject to this kind of identity fraud. When Mike was in law school, he was lost (in fact, it was being lost that drove him to law school in the first place). Rather than doing the hard work of figuring out how he would use the gift and privilege of the education he was receiving, Mike decided to strive for the same golden ring as almost everyone else and got a corporate law job in a big firm. It took him years to figure out that this wasn't what he wanted, and even more to figure out what to choose for himself. If you're like Mike and haven't figured it out, now is a good time to start the process of articulating your identity.

> Only 28% of people feel like they are actively shaping the narrative of their life.

NPCs, Pawns, and Wantons

Although the video game labels of NPCs and Main Characters may be new, the ideas that underlie these concepts have been studied for decades. Back in 1968, educational psychologist Richard de Charms used the terms *Origin* and *Pawn* to connote the distinction between free and forced. According to de Charms's theory, "An Origin is a person who perceives his behavior as determined by his own choosing; a Pawn is a person who perceives his behavior as determined by external forces beyond his control."[3] Distinguishing between intrinsic and extrinsic motivation, de Charms believed that humans are constantly trying to be the cause of their own behavior, fighting against external forces.[4]

Adding to the conversation, Harry Frankfurt, an American philosopher, argued in 1988 that personhood isn't an automatic trait. It doesn't belong to anyone with a mind; rather, personhood is a concerted effort to decide which desires to act on.[5] To him, the difference between humans and animals here anything more than humans' ability to structure their will. Frankfurt's version of NPCs, which he calls "wantons," are able to act on desires but unable to decide which desires to act on.

Finding Our Pools of Will

Much like Frankfurt's wantons, many workers no longer know what they really want. Like the proverbial frog in boiling water, employees' agency—their ability to live their lives the way they want to—has slowly decreased as lean management, just-in-time processes, and checklists have become more and more popular. By reducing the choices available to employees, corporations reduce variety, and the theory goes, increase productivity. But all of this comes at the cost of the workers' ability to make their own choices, all to the benefit of overarching corporate goals.

Disengaged workers go along with the ebbs and flows, acting on what they've been told to want and living their intentional lives outside of work. This theme was taken to the extreme by the 2022 sci-fi psychological thriller series *Severance*, in which workers voluntarily submit to a procedure that severs their work life from their personal life. Today's workers trade their freedom of choice for wages and agree to act in accordance with the intentionality of their employer. This isn't shared intentionality. Here, the choices are made for you, not with you.

But it's possible to live in a system of shared intentionality and still be a Main Character. Many philosophers believe these two ideas are not only highly compatible, but mutually reinforcing. As British philosopher Margaret Gilbert explains, "When a goal has a plural subject, each of a number of persons (two or more) has, in effect, offered his will to be part of a pool of wills which is dedicated, as one, to that goal."[6] Shared intentionality cannot be imposed or transactional; it must arise voluntarily from shared belief. If we're intentional about which pools of wills we're willing to contribute to, our goals can remain our own and still be part of a collective. This is the balance or mutuality that nourishes a Main Character.

The Power of Responsibility

In today's complex business environment, the ability to take responsibility and make decisions is becoming more and more important.[7] Unfortunately, many of us make choices for all the wrong reasons at work (and in our personal lives): blindly following someone else's decisions, protecting our roles, or managing expectations in order to avoid risk and "cover our asses."

A friend of ours, a senior executive recruiter in the retail industry, has spent a decade looking for North America's most capable leaders. She explained to us that plenty of applicants come from top universities and have super-achiever résumés, but that is not what she is looking for. Interestingly, she claims that the hardest attribute to find isn't knowledge or expertise or even cultural fit. It's finding leaders who are willing to take responsibility for company decisions.

Unfortunately, many of us live in corporate environments of accusation, blame avoidance, and de-responsibilization. As a result, top executives don't actually make as many decisions as we may think. Common strategies to avoid making decisions include waiting to see which way the wind blows or blindly (and expensively) following the advice of so-called experts, who are likely to just tell you what you want to hear. The rise of the management consulting industry, now valued at more than $380 billion worldwide, speaks in part to our growing desire to abdicate responsibility to someone else. In a provocative piece in *The New Yorker*, Ted Chiang suggested that the rise of artificial intelligence (AI) will make this even worse—that AI will supplant management consultants as the new repository of blameless responsibility.[8]

Becoming a Main Character in a World of Shared Intentions

In fact, any time we combine with other humans in a shared endeavor, we are required to give up some of our individual intentional power. Of course, freedom has always been limited by the rights and needs of others, but all too often we abandon too much of that freedom because we don't look for and push the limits of what we can decide for ourselves. Like leaders who outsource their decisions, we often choose not to exercise our individual intentional power and submit to the limited choices we are offered but not limited to.

Becoming Main Characters in a world of shared intentionality means making choices. You must create your own intentions and act on them to the extent that you can and then find pools of will that you are happy to contribute to. When you have to participate in a system of imposed intentionality, like work or school, extend your free will as much as you can. Choose a workplace that aligns with your values, or find a school that promotes your own learning style. If you're stuck in a situation where you have limited choices of workplace or school, find the aspects of your job that you can affect, and work toward being able to make bigger decisions.

In the end, we need to find and explore opportunities for expressing our real selves. If you're stuck in a limiting situation, find moments where you can exercise your will. Maybe that's just in how and what you think about. By being intentional about even the smallest of choices, you are moving closer to your true intentions. If you love animals, for instance, but don't have the education or means to land a well-paying job in the animal care industry, you can volunteer or adopt older animals that need end-of-life care. Every intentional choice strengthens our sense of authentic self and pays enormous dividends in terms of our engagement and satisfaction in life.

Life isn't a movie, and there's probably no one momentous choice we can make that will turn us into a Main Character. We can, however, become more skillful at exercising our agency to become liberated from imposed scripts, and simultaneously free to choose who we are and want to be. The next time you find yourself facing a decision, question whether you're prioritizing your own intention. Are you following through on imposed intentionality or on your own personal expression of choice?

At the end of *Free Guy*, Ryan Reynolds has escaped the limitations of being an NPC. He lives in a world called Free Life, excited to be able to do anything he wants, living outside of his previously never-ending loop and inspiring the other NPCs from the game to do the same. While it's simplistic to say that as a Main Character you can do *anything* you want, what is true is that as you become more intentional, you're engaging more with life, and in doing so taking control of who you are. Even if you're just ordering that cappuccino, by becoming a Main Character, you'll find yourself more aligned with who you want to be.

CHAPTER 5

Intention Is Trainable

"The greatest discovery of any generation is that a human can alter his life by altering his attitude."

—William James

Being intentional leads to higher performance, both on an individual and group level. It makes us better (and perhaps more importantly, happier) managers, parents, friends, citizens, and humans because we are more engaged in our lives. And so, the argument for becoming more intentional clearly makes sense, especially since it was also our competitive advantage as a species. However, as we've seen, intention can be a double-edged sword. Our ability to grab onto ideas and execute them can put us in situations where we become slaves to the very things that are meant to express our intention.

This is where we might find people, who have spent their lives chasing status and money, suddenly waking up to the fact that they never wanted those things in the first place. Or people who make decisions to please someone in their life, realizing that nothing they do seems to satisfy that person. The issue isn't that these people are not acting with intention—it's that they've learned to act on someone else's intentions.

On the other end of the spectrum, we may find folks who seem naturally wired to act on their own accord and live with agency. People who are the cause, not the effect. People who live by their own principles and seem to radiate meaning to those around them. Our work

29

and research have shown us that the difference between these two types of people is the same five skills (willpower, curiosity, integrity, attention, and habit formation) that anyone can become adept at.

This fact deserves some pause. The world around us has conditioned us to believe that the extent to which we can live purposeful lives is limited. Limited by who we are, how we were raised, our current circumstances, our social circle, our job, and so on. And yet, an increasing amount of research shows that a sense of agency and purpose aren't things only available to some folks—all of us can predictably build them. Not only that, but in researching this book and seeing the profound effects that these skills can have, we believe that these are things that all of us *should* build. We owe it to ourselves. Not just because it can make us feel better, but because it can help us to be better—to ourselves, to those around us, and as part of a global community struggling to adapt to a world where the pull to automaticity is increasing daily.

Becoming more intentional is not only desirable, it is also very achievable. As surprising as this may seem, we can work on intention, just like we train a muscle. But before we begin focusing on the specifics of training your intention, we need to acknowledge the leap of faith needed. The idea that applying mental effort can somehow unlock higher performance is alluring, which is exactly why it's somewhat hard to believe. To illustrate the strong scientific basis for this, we lay out a few concrete examples from sports, academics, and health, where training intention happens all the time.

Training Intention as a Key to Sports Performance

Imagery is a popular psychological strategy in sports, used to improve performance, mental fortitude, and even rehabilitation from injuries. Imagery is a mental visualization, a repeated practice in which an athlete envisions their chosen task using all five senses. You've likely heard professional athletes explain how they go through everything internally first as a way to prepare themselves to swing a bat or racquet, shoot a free throw, or kick a soccer ball. In professional sports, the use of imagery is commonplace.

An Olympic diver might rehearse walking to the end of a diving board, smelling the chlorine, and feeling the rough board beneath their feet and their cap snug against their head. They would picture their starting position—how it feels, how their muscles move together—their lift-off, their maneuvers through the air, and their graceful entrance into the water. In the lead-up to a competition, they might envision the same sequence hundreds of times.

Numerous studies have examined the effectiveness of imagery practices. In a 2021 meta-analysis, Bianca Simonsmeier and her colleagues looked at studies that compare mental imagery combined with physical exercise to just physical exercise alone, and found that, across the close to 400 studies they looked at, imagery with physical training led to better outcomes than physical training alone.[1] Given that mental imagery is a fairly easy skill to understand, it's surprising how little it's taught in a sports context outside of professional teams.

Imagery is an ideal example of training intention: not only does it improve an athlete's physical performance, it also enhances their mental performance. Dr Jennifer Cumming, a professor of sport and exercise psychology from the University of Birmingham, explains that imagery helps athletes to compete more effectively and get the most out of their training, but it also keeps them motivated and psychologically sharp.[2] As a form of intention, imagery is a tool that requires skill and practice, but it's all in our heads—and that's not a bad thing.

That same meta-analysis from Simonsmeier also found that introducing imagery practices can significantly enhance motivational, psychological, and performance outcomes.[3] Athletes who paired imagery with physical practice did far better than those who only practiced the latter. In other words, imagery didn't just "make up" for lost practice time; it provided its own unique benefits to the athletes. Imagery gave them a leg up—in physical feats, psychological feats, and motivation—that physical practice alone couldn't provide.

Another facet that makes imagery a prime example of training intention is the work it takes to perfect. Imagery can be a difficult skill to be great at:

> Try imagining, in perfect detail and real time, an action you perform regularly. Picture the steps of frying an egg; there are plenty of sensations that we usually don't focus on. Did you remember to account for the feeling of the kitchen floor

beneath your feet, the slight heat on your face? Did you speed up the action as you pictured it? Now try this with an action you do every day and then go do that action. How did it change your approach to it?

Mental imagery takes practice. But like with anything else, you'll reap benefits from starting to practice it, and these will only increase with time. Simonsmeier found that the more intense the imagery training, the more effective it was and the better athletes got at imagery, the better their outcomes were.

Most of us would benefit from expanding our mental rehearsal into full-blown imagery. We might already practice an important or stressful conversation in the shower. However, here, we are talking about adding in sensory details and going through the entire scene in real time.

If you're looking to incorporate imagery into your method for goal-achievement and want to do it in an evidence-aligned way, work your way up to sessions of 20 minutes. Across the 55 studies and 1,438 participants they reviewed, Simonsmeier found that a 20-minute imagery practice session was the sweet spot—no more, no less. You can apply it to your next big pitch presentation, tennis game, or even your next pottery masterpiece. Just remember: it takes practice, so you will need to incorporate imagery into your preparation as an ongoing habit.

Intentions can be so powerful that even when they're distantly separated from the ensuing actions (such as with sports imagery), they can have profound effects on performance. To further illustrate this point, let's look at a slightly different context—school.

Training Intention as a Key to Academic Performance

Not everyone gets the hang of college immediately. There's often a learning curve to the new, self-directed learning that university students are required to undertake. Contrary to what many stressed students might feel, just because a student is struggling doesn't mean they aren't cut out for school. They simply need to get better at it.

But how can individuals get better at school? In a popular meta-analysis, Steven Robbins and others looked at predictors of academic performance across more than 100 different studies.[4] They wanted to see which factors most strongly predict a student's college performance and found that, from all the factors studied, setting very concrete goals and having high self-efficacy were the two most important ones, in other words, setting intentions and then feeling a sense of ability to carry out those intentions. These factors were much better predictors than academic related skills, socioeconomic status, standardized tests, and even high school GPA. The best part? These factors are trainable.

Research like this has popularized approaches in education like social and emotional learning (SEL). These methods place a stronger emphasis on teaching soft skills, like intentional goal setting. While education usually happens at the concrete level (memorizing that *pi* = 3.1416, or the capital of Peru is Lima), most of the value derived from school is at the meta level (learning how to learn and being socialized). Approaches like SEL that promote intentionality carry forward into all aspects of life. They shouldn't be just a nice-to-have add-on to the standard curriculum of math or English. For many students—particularly those who lack role models or have a history of marginalization—these soft skills are the main course.

While SEL has gained popularity (full disclosure, two of this book's authors, Dan and Sekoul, have worked with CASEL, the flagship SEL organization), such approaches have a long way to go to close the soft skill gap in the education system. But as research shows, being intentional and feeling that one can act on those intentions effectively are key ingredients to high academic performance and a highly trainable one.

Training Intention as a Key to Healthier Eating

Eating healthy is hard. In a way, it's also much more directly related to intention than sports or academic performance. In contrast to sports that require physical training or a class that may require a certain knowledge, for those of us fortunate enough to have the resources, there's almost no intermediary between our intentions and the consequences of eating healthy. Despite this, for many of us, it may be one of the most difficult exercises of intention.

Eating healthier for a day, a week, or even a month may be accessible to almost everyone (even with a limited budget or resources, eliminating some unhealthy parts of our diet should be achievable). But, as research shows, in the long run, it becomes a Herculean task. In a meta-analysis spanning dozens of different studies, Mann and colleagues[5] found that one- to two-thirds of dieters regain more weight than they lost on their diet. One of the reasons dieting is so hard is that for all its connection to will, dieting can feel weirdly unintentional, which is to say that dieting feels like a constraint on our will rather than an exercise of it. We need to realize that "I won't do" intentions can be as hard (or harder!) than "I will do" ones.

To understand why this might be, a 2015 study set out to find out what barriers people (in particular, young unemployed people) face when trying to eat healthy.[6] Similar to "revenge bedtime procrastination," the researchers found that a huge driver of eating junk food was the feeling of agency it enabled—something desirable to someone who's unemployed and may otherwise feel "stuck." Young people in these circumstances are caught in a "spiral" that makes eating healthy undesirable because it is perceived as yet another way in which people feel that they're being "told what to do."

So what can we do about this? Luckily, self-efficacy can actually be trained.

Two Italian researchers, Elisabetta Savelli and Federica Murmura, studied what influences the sustained intention to eat healthy in Gen-Zs (people born between the mid-to-late 1990s and the early 2010s).[7] They found that a feeling of self-efficacy was a big predictor of success. However, they also found that this self-efficacy could be built up as a result of strong knowledge about healthy food, including nutritional content, preparation, and seasonality. In other words, while we may not be able to just generate self-efficacy out of thin air, a concerted effort can be made to build its precursors, which can then translate into a long-term feeling of agency.

The point here isn't that learning about different diets like intermittent fasting and keto can help you lose weight—it's that there are pathways to training intention, which can then translate into sustained real-world performance. We dig into how exactly to do that in Chapter 6.

PART II

Willpower

CHAPTER 6

The Surprising Impact of Willpower Attitude

"An alternate view of the world. . .one that recognizes how much of our reality is socially constructed, may actually afford more personal control."

—Ellen Langer

So much of our modern lives seems to rely on willpower. With the onslaught of enticing options and attractive distractions in our overstimulated world, it seems that we're increasingly reliant on our power to act responsibly and resist temptation. Unfortunately, for many of us, relying on willpower is a taxing process. It grinds us down until we eventually have no choice but to give in. Whether it's a long day at work, countless distractions from our digital devices, or the constant demands of daily life, our willpower reserves dwindle. We're left vulnerable to procrastination or indulging in unhealthy habits.

This story of struggling with willpower should be familiar. After all, most people believe that willpower is a limited resource. We therefore need to do everything we can to conserve and preserve it, lest we waste it on pointless tasks and decisions. This is why many "life hackers" encourage us to limit the decisions we have to make by wearing the same clothes every day or eating the same meals. It's why a huge body of self-help literature advises readers to structure their days in a way that puts the toughest decisions first thing in the morning, before our willpower gets all used up. We see our willpower much in the same way we may view the battery power on our smartphone; we only have so much, and it's not always possible to recharge when we're running low.

All of this makes perfect sense. Or at least it used to make sense. Now, a new science of willpower has challenged the core assumptions behind this common knowledge. And this, it turns out, is very good news for our ability to be more intentional.

The Birth of Limited Willpower

The science behind the idea of limited willpower accelerated in the late 1990s, when Roy Baumeister and colleagues published the now-classic "Ego Depletion: Is the Active Self a Limited Resource?"[1] The answer, according to that 1998 team, was yes, and their conclusion was soon amplified by a choir of ensuing studies.

In his ego depletion study, Baumeister tested how long students would work to complete a puzzle after eating either warm chocolate chip cookies or cold, spicy radishes. The kicker was that both groups were exposed to both snacks. The unfortunate students selected for the radish-eating group smelled the enticing aroma of fresh-baked cookies but had to resist them. Baumeister found that students who were permitted to eat the cookies tried to complete the puzzle task for an average of 19 minutes. They hadn't exerted any willpower trying to resist the cookies; their willpower tanks were full. But the students who had to resist the temptation of fresh cookies? They only tried to solve the puzzle for a lowly 8 minutes on average before giving up.

Thus, the theory of ego depletion was born. A couple of decades later, it had been replicated in hundreds of studies around the world. Researchers have found that ego depletion leads to a plethora of undesirable behaviors. It turned out that once our willpower reserves deplete, we become worse versions of ourselves. Ego depletion makes us less likely to help others.[2] It makes us more vulnerable to impulsive behaviors, like alcohol consumption.[3] It can negatively impact athletic performance by affecting exercise-related behaviors and routine.[4] It was even found in dogs, where self-control depletion led to aggressive behavior.[5] Ego depletion became one of the most cited psychological phenomena ever.[6]

The limited nature of willpower, for all intents and purposes, was a fact. At least for a very long and defining moment that still echoes into our lives.

Our society latched onto these findings about ego depletion and limited willpower, suggesting that the same applied in everyday life. Whole generations were granted moral license to relax after they met their daily quota of self-control. Have you had a full day of work, sat through a boring presentation, or tried to withhold your emotions? You're at your limit—there's only so much you can do in a day and so you can be excused from trying to do more or control yourself.

Shifting the Willpower Narrative

But then in 2014, a 23-year-old graduate student at the University of Miami found something strange. Like many others before, Evan Carter set out to replicate one of the core facets of ego depletion. He collected one of the biggest samples in the history of ego depletion literature. To his astonishment, he was unable to replicate the effect.

Carter was convinced he had carried out the experiment incorrectly, as he explained in a rare interview.[7] But after reviewing the literature with his advisor, a whopping 281 studies and experiments, and using top-of-the-line analytical techniques, the two found "very little evidence" supporting ego depletion.

The theory of ego depletion now had the first nail in its coffin: the evidence wasn't there for the most part, and when it was there, it was very weak. It turned out that what looked like a very rigorous effect replicated around the world was, according to Carter and his team, probably the result of publication bias. Perhaps not surprisingly, psychologists were more likely to publish experiments with exciting results, not the ones that failed to show evidence of ego depletion. When controlling for this type of bias, Carter and his researchers found that there was only a small and nonsignificant ego depletion effect.

Rarely have entire fields seen this magnitude of shift. Social psychology was turned on its head. To be fair, we believe that

Baumeister was probably tapping into something significant, but his findings were not clearly identifying it.

With the status quo upheaved, research investigating other theories of willpower burgeoned. Researchers increasingly found evidence against the idea of a finite, diminishing reserve of self-control. However, many psychologists still argued that there was an effect. Indeed, a large body of literature found some semblance of ego depletion in a variety of contexts. What exactly was going on?

While the debate is still ongoing, a new theory began to emerge, led by researchers like Anirban Mukhopadhyay, Gita Johar, and Veronika Job. An increasing amount of research started to show that ego depletion wasn't an all-or-nothing concept, but a variable construct that differed from person to person. While some people believe that they have limited willpower, other people simply believe the opposite: either that their willpower is unlimited or perhaps that no such thing as willpower even exists. What really struck these researchers was that ego depletion was a real effect—*but only in those who believed in the limited nature of willpower.* Individuals who did not have these beliefs just didn't show the same effects—their willpower reserves wouldn't get depleted in the same way.

In a 2010 paper aptly titled "Ego Depletion—Is It All in Your Head?" Veronika Job and her Stanford research team explored the extent to which these findings carried over into the real world.[8] In the longitudinal portion of the experiment, the team showed that people's beliefs about willpower could not only predict whether ego depletion affected them but also seemed to predict other things. People who believed in nonlimited willpower showed better eating behavior, less procrastination, and better goal-striving.

This was groundbreaking and exciting news. Further studies confirmed that those who didn't buy the story of limited willpower showed better self-regulation, in the laboratory and also in their real lives. Students who didn't believe in limited willpower got higher grades.[9] A Swiss-German team even found that kindergarteners who don't think of willpower (in 5-year-olds' parlance) as limited showed better self-regulation than the 5-year-olds who thought their willpower was limited.[10] It turns out that what we believe makes a real, measurable difference in our performance. Or as Henry Ford put it: "Whether you think you can, or you think you can't—you're right." The limits we impose on ourselves have much more profound effects than we think.

How Tired Are You, Really?

By now, it might sound like we're crossing a boundary, suggesting that the only thing holding us back is our mindset. That physical and mental limits are myths brought about by dubious science. But that is not what we are saying. Of course, humans have very real limits. We can't keep going forever, no matter how much drive we have powering us. We're still limited by the laws of physics, our glycogen reserves, how much more tension that muscle fiber can take, and so on. And many of us are limited by our physical abilities, disease, and other factors outside of our control. But the key is that we may not be the best judges of where those limits actually are.

In 2022, researchers from Harvard published a study titled "The Fatigue Illusion: The Physical Effects of Mindlessness." They argued that while we take fatigue to be a mental representation of a physiological state, this is actually an illusion. Instead of giving us an accurate reading, our subjective feeling of fatigue is actually more of a protective mechanism to keep us from wasting energy. And since we rarely, if ever, encounter our actual physical limits, we take this subjective measure to be reality for our entire lives. Only people who have scratched the surface of real physical limits can attest to this. As David Goggins, an ultramarathoner and former Navy SEAL, has put it: "When you think that you are done, you're only 40% into what your body's capable of doing. That's just the limits that we put on ourselves."[11] Far from the level of Navy SEALs, but Mike learned this when he was in the Black Watch, an Army Reserve Regiment in Canada. What he found was that during long training sessions your unwillingness to let your platoon down would force you to push far past the point where your mind was telling you to stop. And in doing so, you found that sometimes your mind plays tricks on you. That's why runners often log their best times in races rather than in perfect training conditions when they're out by themselves. The excitement and pressure of a group of people running beside you helps push you past what you think your limits are.

It turns out our notion of fatigue is less a representation of actual energy reserves and more of a story we like to tell ourselves. Perhaps, as the authors of the fatigue illusion study suggest, our tiredness is often actually a sociocognitive construct based on a combination of task expectations, past experiences, and social cues. This effect is so strong that, as the study found, our fatigue milestones vary during a task depending on the length of the task. In other words, if we expect a task to be hard and long, we start to feel fatigued after more effort has been expended. For example, if you're going on a two-hour drive, then you'll feel the same level of fatigue after one hour (the midway point) as someone who is going on a four-hour drive will feel after two hours.

This feels counterintuitive. But it makes sense when you consider how we evolved. Fatigue is more than just an "FYI." Like pain, it's an evolutionary mechanism that protects us from unnecessary risks and preserves energy reserves for times we might really need them.

Willpower acts in a somewhat similar fashion, but for whatever reason, it doesn't seem to be hard-coded—some people believe willpower is limited, and some people do not. Most important for our purposes, that belief can be trained.

Seeing through the Limited Willpower Illusion

While our beliefs about willpower can influence how much self-control we exert, it's easy to challenge the direction of that causality. A skeptic might think that those who exhibit more willpower in these experiments are simply high performers. They were born with more willpower, and as a consequence, believe they have unlimited amounts of it. Perhaps, the argument might conclude, this whole correlation between willpower theories and exhibited willpower is a fluke caused by a few pesky high achievers. But research shows this isn't the case.

For one, that same fatigue study we just referred to experimented with altering perceptions of fatigue. They instructed participants to use mindfulness to get a better sense of how fatigued they really were. One kind of mindfulness was surprisingly effective at overcoming the fatigue illusion. This was Langerian mindfulness—a concept introduced by Harvard psychologist Ellen Langer that focuses on paying close attention to the novelty of the present moment.[12] By treating each moment more explicitly as unique and important, we can reduce the effect that those sociocognitive factors play in the fatigue illusion. The same is true for willpower attitudes.

In a fascinating 2012 study[13] by Eric Miller, Veronika Job, Carol Dweck and others, researchers randomly assigned participants to "limited" and "nonlimited" willpower groups. They manipulated people's implicit theories about willpower through questionnaires designed to lead them to one of two conclusions (willpower is limited or it isn't). Participants were then asked to do a tedious 20-minute task, repeating the same thing more than 500 times. What they found was striking. While the two groups didn't differ in accuracy in the first half of the task, they found that those in the nonlimited willpower group improved significantly during the second half. Those who were placed in the limited willpower group didn't improve at all.

Studies like this demonstrate that willpower isn't just linked to our beliefs, but that our beliefs can also be trained to unlock more self-control. And this isn't particularly difficult training. It requires practicing mindfulness about where your sense of limited willpower comes from. Is it a real indication that you "can't" go on? Are you really so worn out after work that you cannot possibly force yourself to get up and go to the gym, or resist buying those cookies? While these feelings might be real to you, research suggests they're largely made up. Knowing this empowers us to challenge our limits through simple mindfulness checks like the Langerian method of tuning in to the uniqueness and novelty of the moment. Let's be careful here— we're not saying that you should never take breaks, but do so with intention, not because your default setting is to sit down. Experiment with pushing yourself a bit harder, but not to the point where you hurt yourself.

As much as our perception of the world feels real, cognitive science shows us that our minds construct a world in a way that is useful, not accurate. Sometimes the two overlap, other times not. On the one hand, we have extremely accurate representations of our environment that allow us to navigate it and change it in ways that suit us. On the other hand, we are prone to various cognitive biases, including the willpower and fatigue illusions we just discussed. These biases try to be helpful, but in many situations they place unnecessary limits on us. While our ancestors were probably better off eating high-calorie foods whenever they were available and not going for a 10K run after a long day of chasing mammoths, we live in a very different world. In order to survive and thrive in this world, we are well advised to shed some of those biases and unlock our true potential. Chances are, we'll thank ourselves later.

CHAPTER 7

High Performers Have Nonlimited Willpower

"I am not afraid of storms, for I am learning how to sail my ship."

—Louisa May Alcott

Our story here begins with someone you might never have heard of: Warren Harding. We don't mean the 29th U.S. president, although it would be funny if it was the same Warren Harding. This Warren Harding was one of the most influential rock climbers of all time. Throughout the 1950s, 1960s, and 1970s, he revolutionized and even co-created the sport. He was the first person to ascend El Capitan, a 3,600-foot granite monolith that towers over Yosemite National Park. At the time he did this, in 1958, most considered it to be an impossible feat. El Capitan was too tall, the granite was too slippery, and the climb would take way too long.

This was the 1950s, so wall climbing was still in its infancy. The limits of the sport hadn't yet been tested. Like in any sport, climbs that many amateurs can accomplish today were considered world-class back then. But this doesn't hold true for El Capitan: it's still considered to be one of the most difficult climbs in the world, over 60 years later.

At the time, Harding—also known as Batso due to his uncanny ability to hang off walls—was a young man looking for a challenge.

He took up mountaineering because, as he put it: "It was the first thing I was ever good at. I couldn't catch a ball or any of that stuff. I could only do what required brute stupidity."[1]

Whether it was brute stupidity or just a suspension of disbelief, a unique point of view was a prerequisite given just how much more difficult this climb was compared to other climbs of that era. In preparation, Harding and his climbing party approached everything methodically. They spent months studying the face of the mountain and plotting a course. Finally, he set out with two other climbers to make an attempt.

The climb, which takes multiple days and requires supplies to camp on the rock face, was even more difficult than any of them anticipated. After a few days, one of the climbers decided to turn back due to sheer exhaustion. Harding refused to yield. He continued upward, camping out on tiny ledges and living off barely any food at all. His supporters watching him were horrified—crews on the ground even made attempts to rescue the climbers. Harding turned each of them away.

Harding made his way slowly upward until he finally reached an overhanging section that seemed impossible to traverse. The obvious solution was to stop, train, come back next season and try again. Harding persisted, spending days learning how to do each minute move on the section. His exhaustion reached its peak, and he was unsure whether the traverse was humanly possible. He kept trying.

After countless attempts on that overhang, on November 12, 1958, Harding achieved the impossible. He had climbed the "unclimbable" El Capitan. As he reached the top, he let out an elated cry. The entire climb had taken him 45 days.

While many enthusiasts have gone on to climb El Capitan, it stands as one of the most difficult athletic feats, and perhaps the best climb in the world. It has claimed the lives of more than 20 people in the last century. Its tricky, awe-inspiring terrain has turned it into a symbol of human achievement—to the climbing community and beyond. Harding didn't see it that way, though. As he later said, "Looking back, I don't think of my ascents as any great works of art; they were more scratching and clawing your way upward, like a bug in a toilet bowl."

> When asked for the biggest barrier to accomplishing difficult goals, the most common answer is a lack of willpower.

Finding Our Real Limits

As is discussed in Chapter 6, high performers tend to have something in common: they don't view willpower as a limited resource. Perhaps they don't think about willpower at all. Whichever it is, this attitude gives them the ability to push onward when others might give up—not because they're breaking through some sort of internal limit, but because they're too absorbed with the task to pay attention to self-imposed limits in the first place.

That's not to say that physical limits don't exist. As you can tell from Harding's historic climb, rock climbing can push people to real physical limits—of grip strength, stamina, finger tendons, and so on. However, pushing these physical limits requires going far beyond most people's self-imposed mental limits and breaking free of what our mind thinks our potential is.

We chose rock climbing as an example in this chapter because, like other extreme sports, it has a strange ability to lure people away from any notion of willpower. The constant struggle against gravity combined with the real sense of danger means that if you want to progress, you have to break free from any previous understanding of what you can achieve. The result is something that climbers call "try hard": an elusive concept that means pushing yourself beyond your comfortable limit until you reach your actual limit.

As Eric Horst eloquently puts it in his book *Maximum Climbing*:

> With regular mental exercise, you will gradually discover a higher level of consciousness in which you climb with single-pointed focus, detachment from concerns about results, and unstoppable confidence and willpower. This rare state will give birth to experiences that transcend the ordinary and reveal your true potential to do great things. Like wielding a sword with empty hands, your mind will lead your body to new summits. The profound experience that unfolds—in which thought and action merge in a powerful and transcending union—is what maximum climbing is all about.[2]

The concept of "real limits" isn't reserved for top athletes. Even amateur climbers learn to "try hard" in order to progress. And while physical results differ dramatically based on people's bodies, experience, and age, the mental results of trying hard are quite similar: a complete application of resources to the task at hand.

Willpower Can Make Anyone a High Performer

High performance doesn't need to be done in an arena with supporters cheering you on. We can apply the practices of high performance to our day-to-day lives, whether we're learning how to drive or pushing ourselves to read more often. We may apply these practices in situations where we have support, and at times, we might be alone in our journeys. Not everyone has the privilege of positive role models or support from loved ones.

For some, it takes the form of climbing a mountain for the world to see. For others, it might mean quite literally digging through a mountain as an ultimate expression of grief.

Dashrath Manjhi was a poor laborer from Bihar, an eastern state in India on the border of Nepal. In the late 1950s, his pregnant wife suffered a horrendous fall from a mountain in their district. Despite rushing her as quickly as possible to the closest hospital on the other side of the mountain, she was declared dead on arrival.

Manjhi was devastated. Rather than retreating, however, he decided to apply himself to make sure this would never happen to anyone again. He knew it was the long route to the hospital that led to the death of his wife. His village was in an alpine region where long, winding routes circumvented the mountains. Armed with just a simple hammer and chisel, he chipped away at the mountain that sat between his town and the hospital. Slowly, year by year, he carved a pass through the mountain, making it wide enough to accommodate cars.

The road took him 22 years. 22 years! And his feat wasn't originally met with support. He faced ridicule early on from those in his village. As he later reported, the taunting only strengthened his resolve.[3] When he finally finished, he had reduced the distance it took to get to the hospital from 35 miles (56 km) to 10 miles (16 km). His road still stands today, at 360 feet (110 m) long and 30 feet (9 m) wide.

What this story illustrates is that high performance isn't about having innate higher limits than other people—it's about pushing yourself beyond what you think are your own limits, whatever they may be, and achieving what is important to you, whatever that is. Judging ourselves because we haven't won an NBA championship or launched a billion-dollar business misunderstands the definition of *high performance*. Even worse, it leads us to misunderstand the true challenge of life.

What can Warren Harding's comment about a bug in a toilet bowl and Dashrath Manjhi—or as he's come to be known, the Mountain Man—tell us about willpower? Perhaps that willpower isn't about the result at all. It's about our relationship with ourselves.

Make Your Next Challenge a Test of Willpower

Research supports this idea that willpower reflects how we see ourselves. In a Stanford study by psychologists Eran Magen and James Gross,[4] participants were asked to squeeze a hand dynamometer for as long as they could. Half were told that this is a test of willpower, while the others weren't told anything. The group that had the willpower construal of the task was able to hold the dynamometer for more than 50% longer than the control group. In other words, when the test was framed as a challenge of character, people stepped up.

Next, the researchers wanted to see if the group of people who underperformed would improve when they were told to focus on willpower. They did. It wasn't that some participants had better grip strength than others. Any participant who was challenged to dig into their willpower was able to improve their results substantially.

Magen and Gross didn't just observe this in physical strength. In the last phase of their experiment, participants were asked to perform an attention task while being distracted with funny videos. But those who were told it was a test of willpower, instead of a plain old test, paid more attention to the task at hand. In a conversation with Dr. Gross, he told us that what he sees as the take-home message from this work is that "valuing willpower and seeing a context as relevant to this value yields increased willpower."[5] In a reaction to his own findings and understanding, Dr. Gross also told us that he used to read Epictetus's *Enchiridion*, a short manual on how to live compiled in the 2nd century, to his kids when they were young to instill in them this fundamental concept: most of our limitations are self-imposed.[6]

In other words, in many cases, what might seem like hard limits can be overcome by applying a deeper sense of awareness to the situation. We don't believe that willpower is some sort of special resource that can only be activated when you think about it. Rather, we believe that we are hard-wired to place unconscious limits on ourselves, and shining a light on those limits helps us to realize they're not real. This is an important point that we'll return to.

Define Your Limits

Even after hearing the evidence on the power of a nonlimited willpower mindset, it's easy to fall back on our old, self-imposed limitations.

> Imagine two scenarios: one in which willpower is a limited resource and one in which it is nonlimited. In the first, your ability to be intentional and live toward your goals is limited by the quantity of willpower that you have. In the second, only external circumstances are in the way of you achieving your goals. Now project that difference into your own life. Imagine a year of living without willpower limits. What could you achieve? What about if you could live the rest of your life like this?

Author Michael Singer provides a good example of this in *The Michael Singer Podcast*.[7] Imagine you're an addicted smoker. You've tried and failed to quit multiple times. You believe you don't have the willpower to stop. The willpower to resist picking up one more cigarette would be incredibly hard. It might even feel impossible.

But imagine that you know that the cigarette—laying ominously in front of you—is laced with arsenic. The instant you take a puff, you're on your way to a speedy, unpleasant death. Resisting suddenly seems a lot easier. Almost all of us could resist an arsenic cigarette. This means that your willpower is able to do more heavy-lifting than you think.

Don't get us wrong; this isn't easy, and there's no need to hustle 24/7. In fact, there's absolutely nothing wrong with sitting on your couch and watching that flashy new series. The question is whether we're able to make intentional choices or are we operating in default mode? Can we resist these things when we have other, more important objectives? Is it bad that you're watching an old season of *Real Housewives*? No. Is it bad that you're watching it when you haven't started on the homework you have due tomorrow? Probably.

Fortunately, *you* make these choices. What's even better is that you have the willpower necessary to make the best choices. All you need to do is believe (or know) that you do.

And like any other mental skill, our self-regulation can be trained. One study of self-control demonstrated that people who were trained in meditation for over 19,000 hours showed more activity in brain regions associated with self-control, like the dorsolateral prefrontal cortex.[8] Nonmeditators showed greater activity in regions associated with temptation, like the ventromedial prefrontal cortex and the anterior cingulate cortex.

The study's third group were people who had recently started meditating. These folks had intermediate levels of activity in the regions that indicated self-control, demonstrating the increasing benefits of meditation over time. Self-regulation, this shows, can be trained.

So, even though behavioral skills like self-regulation can feel set in stone, they aren't anything we can't change. All it takes is the dedication to stick with it—in other words, willpower. But even before that, we need to learn that training these behavioral skills is completely possible.

There is also another level of self-mastery here that is important to recognize. The benefits of exploring our potential and pushing our limits aren't limited to climbing mountains, resisting cigarettes, or doing higher quality homework. When we push our self-imposed limitations, we get the benefit of knowing that we can go beyond our self-imposed limitations. We're all capable of overcoming our self-imposed limits—and it feels oh so good to do so.

The great news here is that we have more willpower than we think. The bad news? That finding shifts the onus back onto us. Embracing this responsibility is a good first step to living intentionally. Within the circumstances we're given (which admittedly for some people can be very limiting and challenging), we're the only ones responsible for how our lives turn out relative to those circumstances. The sooner we embrace that reality, the sooner we can start living with intention. And as further incentive, we should know that the first "wins" may be the most difficult. Once we have the experience of overcoming ourselves, so to speak, we will more automatically consider the very real possibility that the mountain in front of us is largely in our mind.

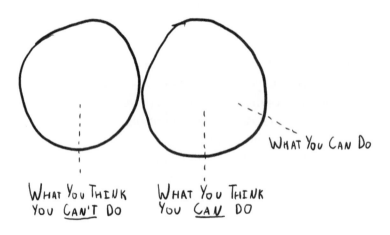

WHAT YOU THINK   WHAT YOU THINK   WHAT YOU CAN DO
YOU CAN'T DO   YOU CAN DO

CHAPTER 8

Physical Ingredients to Willpower

"The only way of finding the limits of the possible is by going beyond them into the impossible."

—Arthur C. Clarke

You're at the tail end of a long day at work. It was made particularly heavy by an endless barrage of meetings and a skipped lunch. You started off really strong this morning. You got a good night's sleep, and you were ready for anything. But with each meeting, you can feel your self-control gently slipping. You were going to pass by the gym on the way home, but that's starting to feel increasingly unlikely. After all, you're exhausted and hungry. It's unlikely you'll be able to muster the self-control to get through a workout, so why force it?

It's fairly common knowledge that our basic physiological states, such as hunger or lack of sleep, can limit our willpower. But, as we saw with other willpower myths, common sense isn't always right. While physiological factors do influence our performance, new research tells us that the link between these factors and our willpower might be more in our heads than we thought. In this chapter we look at some physical factors in human performance that are assumed to be fixed so that we can figure out what is actually true. What we believe, as we have just read, has a powerful effect on what we can achieve.

As is noted in previous chapters, conventional ideas about willpower have been challenged in recent years. The scientific community once accepted that willpower was a finite resource, one that could be depleted. But new evidence suggests this effect is dampened when we choose not to conceive of willpower as limited. What we thought was a physiological feature of our bodies may be, in part, a sociocultural construct—something we're taught to believe that places unnecessary limits on us.

Does Being Hungry Make You Lose Self-Control?

Let's go back to 10th-grade biology for a second. As you might remember, our brains are powered by glucose, a type of sugar we get from carbohydrate-rich foods like fruit and bread. We rely on glucose to function—glucose levels can affect things like mood, memory, and learning. For a long time, our levels of glucose, which are a good measure of how hungry we feel, have also been associated with variations in self-control. But while many believe that willpower is dependent on glucose levels, research shows that this is unlikely to be the case. We need glucose to function in other ways, but not to exert willpower.

A 2002 study in *Nutrition Research Reviews* explains the historical link between glucose and cognitive functions. Most research on the two had assumed that since glucose powers our brains, the level of glucose in our blood would impact the level of glucose in our brains, and thus, our neuronal functions. "However," the researchers caution, "the strength of this notion lies in its common-sense plausibility, not in scientific evidence."[1]

The link between glucose and willpower has been shown in multiple studies. At the same time, other studies have shown that our brains don't consume extra glucose when exerting effort, like memory or coping with stress.[2,3,4] So, on the one hand, glucose seems to allow us to exert self-control. On the other hand, it isn't actually used for self-control. How can this be?

The answer lies in the power of belief—not in some fluffy sense, but in the very real sense that changes how our brains perceive reality. Believing in the helpful effects of glucose may be why it's helpful to us. In a study led by Dr. Veronika Job, a motivational psychologist at the University of Vienna, participants were asked to perform a test of self-control: the Stroop task.[5] In this classic psychology test, participants must quickly read through a list of colors, naming not the colors they're reading, but the color of the words. In some conditions, it's easy—like identifying the color green when the word is *green*. But it's surprisingly hard to say the color of the word, rather than its name (like saying orange and not green, when you see "green" written in orange). This gets especially challenging when you're doing it as a speed test. Look it up, and give it a shot if you don't believe us. The difficulty of the Stroop task makes it an ideal method to test participants' self-control.

The researchers wanted to see whether glucose had an effect on how participants performed the Stroop task. They gave half of the participants glucose and the other half an artificial sweetener, ensuring no one knew which group they were in. As expected from previous research, they saw that glucose significantly increased self-control, whereas the artificial sweetener did not. Surely this was proof of a deep physiological link between glucose and self-control?

Weirdly enough, no. When the researchers looked at people's willpower attitudes, they saw that the glucose effect was only present in people who believed in limited willpower. In other words, people who believed in nonlimited willpower were unaffected by the glucose; they performed well with or without it. For fans of *The Matrix*, there was no spoon—the effect was all in their heads.

Remember, no one could tell whether they'd been given glucose or artificial sweetener. Whatever signals the participants used to determine how much self-control they had left were physiological signals—ones based on the body's internal measure of blood glucose. But these physiological signals had different effects based on the participants' personal beliefs.

As the researchers explained, their study showed "that a seemingly basic physiological process, the effect of glucose ingestion on self-control, depends on cultural beliefs about the nature of willpower."[6] Our thoughts can significantly impact our bodily processes—and our belief in willpower does just that. Read that passage again, as this is something to really pay attention to, and the evidence is not in this study alone.

In follow-ups to the Stroop task study, participants were taught to have either a limited or nonlimited willpower attitude. The effect of glucose—previously thought of as a purely physical reaction—could be manipulated at will by the researchers, depending on which information they gave the participants. All they had to do was make participants believe they had nonlimited willpower, and they did.

Of course, this isn't to say that glucose isn't important to human functioning. It absolutely is, and we would die without it. It just means that while other aspects of our mental performance such as memory and learning might actually be powered by glucose, willpower does not seem to be. Research like this should make us rethink the narrative we tell ourselves after that long day full of meetings and a skipped lunch. It also raises the question of what willpower actually is and whether it's even real. (Spoiler: you may have your beliefs challenged as we explore this possibility.)

Re-thinking Drowsy Days at Work

We've all had the misfortune of sleep-deprived days at work. Whether you were up studying, your kid was up sick, or you had a wild Thursday night out on the town, you drag yourself out of bed the next day and add an extra shot of espresso to your morning coffee to make it through the day.

Since a lack of sleep is more difficult to fix than a lack of food (it's much easier to grab a snack in the middle of the workday than to take a nap), it's a key discussion point for productivity at work. One night of poor sleep can ruin an entire day's work. And a lot of us have trouble getting enough sleep: according to the Centers for Disease Control and Prevention, more than one-third of adults don't get enough sleep on a regular basis.[7]

It's natural to be less productive after a bad night of sleep. In fact, insufficient sleep has been estimated to have an economic loss of over $411 billion each year in the United States alone.[8] But new research is challenging how much of our poor performance is due to a lack of sleep, and how much is influenced by our beliefs.

> More than 60% of people believe that their willpower is influenced by sleep.

Professor Wladislaw Rivkin, who teaches organizational behavior at Trinity College Dublin, found that even drowsiness is changed by our willpower attitudes.[9] In two studies with more than 200 participants, Rivkin and his colleagues found that the amount of time we sleep affects us in three ways at work: our self-control, our emotions, and our motivation.

They found that willpower attitude modulates these effects, just like Job's findings for glucose and self-control. Those who believed in nonlimited willpower had significantly less correlation between their levels of sleep and their effectiveness at work. Limited sleep impacted their day less than those who believed it would. For those who expected a poor night of sleep to negatively impact their day, it did—more than it would have otherwise. In other words, however participants believed a lack of sleep would affect them, they were right.

As with glucose, the point here is not that sleep is unimportant. We're not all-powerful beings who can choose to subsist on a few hours of sleep thanks to sheer willpower, and bad sleep hygiene has been linked to all sorts of negative outcomes such as heart disease, kidney disease, high blood pressure, diabetes, stroke, obesity, and depression. When we spoke with Rivkin, he said these kinds of extreme interpretations are the biggest challenge when the team shares its findings.[10] Many respond with (rightful) skepticism to the finding that nonlimited willpower beliefs can replace our requirements for sleep.

"What is important in my view," he explained, "is to not mis-understand our results in terms of thinking that unlimited beliefs compensate for the lack of sleep." Instead, his results suggest that those who believe that their willpower can be depleted are more focused on their lack of resources after a bad night's sleep. In response to their belief about having too few resources to reach a normal level of productivity, they withheld effort in order to save their precious limited resources. "We're not saying that if you believe in a nonlimited resource theory it allows you to forgo sleep. Rather, it makes you more resilient in coping with a lack of sleep, as it reduces the tendency to save resources." Remember that David Goggins quote from Chapter 6? "When you think that you are done, you're only 40% into what your body's capable of doing. That's just the limits that we put on ourselves."[11] That extra 60% you're protecting is what you can access if you change what you believe your limits to be. And there's no need to use it all, even if we can tap into a small amount of what our mind is holding back, we'll see tremendous results.

The effects of belief differences in willpower limits are apparent when we compare cultural differences between nations. One of Rivkin's interests within his field is the difference in beliefs about sleep between Western and Eastern cultures. If you compare the sleeping habits of Canadian and Japanese university students, Japanese students sleep far less.[12] But despite their extra sleep, Canadian students report being more tired and having worse health than their Japanese counterparts. "People in Eastern cultures may not consider the lack of sleep as an issue," Rivkin explained. "Whereas people in Western cultures tend to agree with a limited willpower theory, people in Eastern countries tend to agree more with a nonlimited theory." In other words, it's not magic. It's just the wildly influential nature of our minds.

Is Willpower Even Real?

Going back to a question we raised earlier—how can beliefs about willpower somehow modulate the effect of physiological cues? We raised this question in an interview with Dr. Judson Brewer, director at Brown University's Mindfulness Center, and *New York Times* bestselling author of books such as *Unwinding Anxiety* and *The Craving Mind*.[13] Brewer is a leading expert on addiction—particularly in the contexts of overeating and smoking. As both a researcher and a clinician, he has had a chance to develop theories and then test them in real patients with very impressive results. This puts him in a unique position to understand concepts such as willpower from both a theoretical and practical point of view. In our wide-ranging discussion with him, Brewer explained to us that the existence of ego-depletion, and even willpower itself, are actually quite difficult to justify based on recent evidence.

> Several meta-analyses of ego-depletion suggest that there is likely a lot of publication bias leading to an overestimation of effect size, which could in fact be zero. In fact, I'm not aware of any literature from a neuroscience point of view that supports the notion of willpower. I am not convinced that there is a neuroscientific basis to willpower.[14]

Let's unpack this a little. While willpower may be a helpful way to think about our experience of being human, this does not necessarily mean it's based on real neural mechanisms. In fact, as Brewer points out, there doesn't seem to be a neural counter that tracks how much "self-control" we have left in the way that our body monitors glucose or hydration levels. Of course, for many of us, that counter still exists subjectively. But the fact that the counter isn't one that is physically built into us reinforces the idea that it is our choice.

Looking for Cues

This raises the question: if willpower isn't a fundamental aspect of our machinery, but a human invention, why did we invent it? Some researchers, like Brewer, think that willpower is likely nothing more than a heuristic (a mental shortcut).

> My working hypothesis is that willpower is a heuristic that humans use to confabulate why they did or did not do something. And when you look under the hood, it's driven by very well worked out neuroscientific notions around reinforcement learning that have been around for over 40 years.[15]

In other words, willpower might be the figment of an overactive imagination trying to build a narrative out of a simple reward system that we share with many other animals. Essentially, we think of our behaviors as driven by constants such as willpower because it gives more apparent cohesion to our lives—it makes it easier for us to understand why we do (or don't do) certain things. What is powerful about this realization is that it allows us to think about and use willpower for our own purposes, rather than being ruled by a legacy construct from our days in caves.

An alternative explanation, from Job, is that willpower beliefs make us more sensitive to internal cues. In order to maximize our chances of survival, these internal cues could help us to preserve energy—never a bad idea if you're in the business of surviving.

To see how this might work, let's use an example: Imagine love is a limited resource. There's a finite amount of love you can experience in your lifetime. Even if you don't know what exactly depletes your storage of love, you'll start to develop theories. Maybe you think the number of relationships you've experienced is dwindling your tank, or maybe it's the number of times you've been hurt by others. Not only will you form these links, you'll start paying special attention to them. You might avoid new relationships, or try to hurt others before they can hurt you. Ironically, these could easily become self-fulfilling prophecies—by believing your love is limited, you could end up severely limiting the love you experience. Of course, this would save you energy (and maybe heartbreak), but that doesn't, of course, make it a good idea to adopt this belief.

Now consider our beliefs about willpower. A person who believes in limited willpower is regularly assessing how much they have left to spare. Their belief in the power of physiological inputs, like food or sleep, heightens their attention to these factors. Making people more sensitive to these inputs, and perhaps overestimating them (as is shown in the research on fatigue in Chapter 7) helps preserve energy (presumably for running away from a predator or to stave off starvation).

Instead of pushing along with their day on too-little sleep, they'll focus on their lack of sleep. How tired do they feel? What can they skip out on to make the best use of their limited willpower? How can they most efficiently spread their resources across the day? Perhaps some of this sounds familiar to you for how you cope with a day on too-little sleep.

While it may have helped our ancestors stay alive, this kind of obsession with these cues is counterproductive in today's world. If you finish a long day of work, hungry and tired, you might decide you don't have the willpower to go home and read this book. You may choose to lay on the couch and skip the mental workout, actively moving away from your goal to read more. In doing this, you're confirming your own beliefs about limited willpower.

Instead of assuming that physical cues are a good measure of what we can and can't do, we can start to challenge ourselves. The next time you're low on sugar or on a few hours of sleep, try to imagine that these inputs have no bearing on your performance. You might be surprised how your body rises to the occasion.

In fact, you can try this right now—ask yourself how tired you are on a scale of 1–10. Now spend a few minutes talking yourself out of it—tell yourself you're not tired, think about the preceding research and what it shows. Imagine yourself in a different culture where notions of sleep are also very different. What level are you at now? If you did the work to convince yourself that it's all (or at least partly) in your head, you'll probably notice a pretty big difference in how you feel. That's the power of a nonlimited willpower belief.

The takeaway insight we can apply from these studies is that our beliefs about our performance and willpower can be limiting how we live our lives. Once we unlock these beliefs, we can change how we live in radical ways.

CHAPTER 9

How to Train the Experience of Willpower

"Believe you can and you're halfway there."
—Theodore Roosevelt

Those who believe willpower is nonlimited aren't constrained in the same ways as those who think of willpower as a scarce resource. So the next step, and where the real impact comes in, is training that understanding—training ourselves to view willpower as a nonlimited resource, and in doing so, overcome our limits to achieve more than we thought possible.

How Seeking Novelty Can Replenish Us

To begin this training process, we go back to the example of fatigue. As you might remember, Camparo and her colleagues conducted experiments on the link between mindfulness and fatigue illusion. They wanted to find out whether mindfulness practices could affect participants' perceptions of their own fatigue.[1]

To assess mindfulness, the team used Langerian mindfulness, which as is noted in Chapter 6, is understood as being actively present in the now and being aware of new events, as opposed to relying too much on previously learned categories.[2] A key aspect of Langerian mindfulness is paying attention to novelty by noticing what is different or changing in our environment, keeping us alive to what is happening in the moment. When participating in Langerian mindfulness, participants in Camparo's experiments noticed a change in how they perceived their own fatigue. In fact, the ideas of Langerian mindfulness "offer[ed] individuals control over the timing, amount, and even the experience of fatigue."[3] Future research will be required to understand exactly why this is, but scientists have a theory, and it has to do with how we perceive or interpret what we are doing.

The connection with willpower, Langer argues, is that "an alternate view of the world. . .one that recognizes how much of our reality is socially constructed, may actually afford more personal control."[4] When limited willpower is recognized as a socially constructed reality, the "alternate view of the world" that emerges through the practice of Langerian mindfulness is one in which we have greater control. Let's look at how that can work.

A key aspect of Langerian mindfulness is producing novelty from a situation. Someone practicing this type of mindfulness might, on their weekly route to the grocery store, pay attention to small differences in day-to-day life. They might focus on the birds they can see as they walk by—the different species, how many are in their town at that time of year, and their behavior. Or they might focus on the changes in the trees, the varied etiquette of drivers and cyclists on the road, or the shifts in the clouds or color of the sky. With Langerian mindfulness, no two trips to the grocery store are ever the same—and that's exciting! Or as German psychiatrist Fritz Perls poetically put it: "If you're bored, you're not paying enough attention." Mike uses that quote on his kids all the time—trust us, they love it!

But why does this work for overcoming or avoiding fatigue? Camparo believed that novelty-seeking helped participants control how they looked at a challenging task. By making a task feel new, it also became less fatiguing. That may seem a bit obvious to folks who are easily excited to try new tasks, but what is really interesting is how this can be trained as a skill. As the research shows, becoming adept at practicing this type of mindfulness may even help us replenish energy.

Langerian mindfulness begins with situating your base state. Generally, how mindful are you? We all have different strengths, and some of us are naturally more mindful than others. Tools have been developed to help identify where you fall along the mindfulness spectrum, and the following short questionnaire takes inspiration from multiple Langer Mindfulness Scales.

For each question, rank yourself on a scale of 1 to 7, with 1 being "strongly disagree" and 7 being "strongly agree":

I'm always open to new ways of doing things.

I generate novel ideas.

I have an open mind about everything, even things that challenge my core beliefs.

I always notice what other people are up to.

I am always alert to new developments.

I like to figure out how things work.

I actively seek to learn new things.

I'm very creative.

I find it easy to create new and effective ideas.

I pay attention to the "big picture" context.

Add up your total to find your score between 10 and 70. The higher you score, the more naturally aligned you are with the ideas of Langerian mindfulness. No matter which range your score falls in, however, you can get better at being mindful and present in your everyday life. Like most skills, it's a matter of practice.

Give it a go right now. Get a sense of your baseline energy level. Now look around you for a couple of minutes. What's new in your field of vision? What haven't you really paid attention to before now? What changes do you see from the last time you were here? And what is different with you? Spend some time going over your entire environment to notice as much as you can about what has recently changed. Now check in with yourself—what is your energy level like? How do you feel and what do you notice about yourself as you do the exercise?

Beyond its effect on willpower perceptions, the benefits of increased mindfulness are almost too many to count, but here's a good list to start us off: Mindfulness (not just Langerian, but other forms of mindfulness as well) has been found to improve cognitive abilities;[5] soft skills (i.e., creativity, communication, collaboration, and critical thinking);[6] and alleviate chronic pain, depression, anxiety, and addiction.[7] Why do you think astronauts, in preparation for their space flights, are taught to utilize Langerian mindfulness?[8] Even in a small spacecraft, we can always find things that are novel or changing.

And recent research has cemented the connection to willpower. In 2016, Pagnini, Bercovitz, and Langer found that mindlessness and a perceived lack of control came from the same source.[9] By *mindlessness*, they refer to an overreliance on previously learned paradigms and concepts, which social scientists call categories (disengagement and languishing, anyone?). Mindfulness, on the other hand, is the practice of noticing new things, promoting flexible responses to changing environments. In reviewing multiple studies on the subject, the authors conclude that mindlessness and a lack of perceived control come from the same source: an assumption of rigidity and unchangeableness of the world. We find it fascinating that believing things can't change is translated to not having control and, therefore, not having agency. Just wait until bedtime so we can try to reclaim that agency by refusing to go to sleep! And where is that crappy junk food?

Our perception of whether we're in control can be trained by progressively shifting our attitude to seek and expect novelty. We can increase our feelings of control by looking at problems from new angles, or even purposefully adding humor to our perception. That's all it takes. The secret to shifting our understanding of willpower is about progressively shifting your attitude to be less rigid. To make sure that we fully grasp this, let's see how shifting our attitude can be applied in practice.

Start Small

When training your mind to think about willpower differently, don't start with the hardest tasks first—just like you shouldn't attempt a marathon in January, freshly following your New Year's resolution to start running. Instead, start to train your mind with smaller tasks that slowly, continuously ramp up to larger and harder goals. Just like a muscle is not going to get strong all at once, building our ability to control the feeling of willpower takes time and effort.

Don't worry too much about the level you start with. So long as you do something challenging outside of your normal pattern of behavior, you're on the right path. If you're going to establish a running habit, there's no harm in beginning by taking walks around the block if that's all you can manage. Even that is a huge accomplishment in and of itself! And it's only by starting something hard that you can ramp up your willpower practice. Once you've got that walk around the block down pat and it has become less of a test of your will, try alternating between jogging and walking. If jogging is too big a step to keep up regularly, start even smaller. Jog for 15 seconds for every couple minutes you walk. Again, as long as it's a step forward and a challenge to get yourself to do it, it doesn't matter how long your stride is.

Or maybe you've been putting off cleaning out the garage or the basement. Or even just doing the dishes. Whatever change you want to make that you might feel overwhelmed by, take a very small step to begin with. Get rid of one thing in the basement. Wash one plate. Start very small and let momentum build. Each of these actions will be both an effort around the task itself and a training of your willpower. Especially if when you start to feel a bit overwhelmed you manage to push through that self-imposed resistance level. That's where the real work on your willpower will be found—pushing against your desire to stop, that feeling that you've had too much, and quieting that too-early warning system in your mind. Of course, you should be careful and work your way up to harder challenges, but try pushing yourself a bit and see how you feel.

If you have trouble keeping up your new tests of willpower, dig deep and ask yourself why. If you're resistant to jogging because your shoes don't fit properly, invest in a pair that works better for you. If the basement is too daunting of a task to accomplish alone, enlist some help. No matter the reason, once you identify it, you can start to strategize how to overcome it. Strangely enough, we often argue for our own limitations and can be our own worst enemy when it comes to doing the right thing, so it's helpful to bring that out into the open where we can question ourselves honestly. Awareness and intention are key here.

Small Wins Are Better than Major Losses

What's the point of taking such small steps? The Progress Principle. In their book of the same name,[10] Teresa Amabile and Steven Kramer looked at a set of employees and found that, no matter the position or personality of the employee, the single greatest indicator of their happiness and performance at work was progress. But progress didn't need to come in the form of promotions or awards. It was actually the small daily wins that motivated people to try harder, be more creative, and be happier at work.

Their work, spanning 120,000 work events over the course of a year, explains why small steps are more motivating than large ones. Since humans are by nature risk-averse, our setbacks diminish our motivation more than our success increases it. Amabile and Kramer explain that a manager's greatest task is paving the way for employees to experience minimal setbacks and regularly feel those small wins. Their examples of workplace setbacks include dismissal of ideas, losing ownership over work, or doing work that one is greatly overqualified for.

In a well-known *Harvard Business Review* article, Amabile and Kramer explain that "of all the things that can boost emotions, motivation, and perceptions during a workday, the single most important is making progress in meaningful work."[11] It's not just any work that counts here. "Whether the goals are lofty or modest," the authors explain, "as long as they are meaningful to the worker and it is clear how his or her efforts contribute to them, progress toward them can galvanize inner work life." Progress shouldn't just come in the form of feedback and participation medals. It must genuinely incorporate both the worker and their cause and be meaningful for them.

When we set lofty goals, like running a marathon when we haven't broken a sweat in years, let's face it: we're more likely to fail and injure ourselves in the process. These setbacks can demotivate us from continuing to strive toward our goals at all, so it's always better to set yourself up for small wins than for a major loss.

Good Motivation versus Bad Motivation

Unsurprisingly, motivation is another of the keys to willpower control. But there are different types of motivation, and they're not all equal.

The best for our purposes is internal motivation. This type of motivation comes from within yourself, unlike expectations that are imposed on you. As Ryan and Deci put it in their seminal paper on self-determination theory:

> Comparisons between people whose motivation is authentic (literally, self-authored or endorsed) and those who are merely externally controlled for an action, typically reveal that the former, relative to the latter, have more interest, excitement, and confidence, which in turn is manifest both as enhanced performance, persistence, and creativity.[12]

We're far more likely to excel if we motivate ourselves, rather than relying on external factors. Instead of abdicating the reason why we do something to our bosses' expectations, we need to find within ourselves a reason that our work is worthwhile. Someone flipping burgers in a fast-food chain might realize that they are helping to feed people. A street sweeper is keeping their city clean. Similarly, rather than getting in shape to fit a societal expectation, we should strive to feel good in our bodies. Once we see our own values in our actions, we're more likely to achieve our goals. In fact, a study on weight loss in women found that those who connected to their own autonomy by exploring personal motivations lost significantly more weight over three years than those who were focused on external motivating factors.[13] Our motivation needs to come from within.

Perhaps one of the reasons we struggle so much with willpower these days is all the external motivation-inducing tools readily available to us: habit apps, productivity apps, smartwatches, and personal coaches of all kinds. When we overly rely on these external motivators, we diminish our ability to motivate ourselves. As a consequence, we're unable to build the necessary internal drive to power our intentions. Motivation, at its best, is an inside game.

Productivity Tools Don't Build Willpower

For every task we face in our daily lives, there's a tool for it. If you're struggling to get organized, there are to-do list apps. If you're trying to build good habits, there are habit-tracking tools. And if you're writing a book, you can use a focus app to block out any and all distractions until you get your target number of words down on a page.

But these tools don't train your understanding of willpower. You still need to overcome Poe's "Imp of the Perverse" that is mentioned in Chapter 1: the dangerous desire to self-sabotage.

When lifting weights, many people like to wear gloves or a belt to support their back. Productivity tools are similar. They help to offset certain negative aspects of the challenge—calloused hands or a bad back—but they don't directly help challenge your belief in limited willpower and help build your sense of nonlimited willpower, so use them intentionally and with caution.

Part of the reason productivity tools can be so addictive is the sense of accomplishment they give us. As neuroscientist Claire Wu explained to the BBC, we can start to value these digital rewards over the accomplishments themselves. "A common theme in many apps is a representation of progress, such as badges or hitting a certain number," explains Wu. "But these can start to become more important than the outcome itself—for example, a person might do a workout but not get the expected badge or points, and feel like the whole effort was a waste of time. But really, the workout is much more important than some arbitrary points."[14]

Have you ever met someone committed to taking 10,000 steps each day? Maybe they pace around while on calls, or take an evening walk if they need to reach their daily target. Someone laser-focused on that magic number might be despondent if they forgot to bring along their phone or smartwatch, "wasting" steps that wouldn't count toward their goal. In a *New York Times* article, David Sedaris discussed how he is so obsessed with getting in his 21,000 steps a day such that on one long flight he jogged in his seat to get the steps in![15] Perhaps most emblematic of this mindset are the real-life machines that jiggle your smartwatch to simulate walking. Or Duolingo's offer to repair your lost "streak" if you pay up. In the preceding article cited, Sedaris said that he once paid someone to wear his Apple Watch and walk around for two hours so that he could meet his goal! Once we start to value useless rewards over our original goals, it's time to take a step back and consider what we're really aiming for.

Take Pride in Your Achievements

If you're training your conception of willpower, you might as well enjoy it. Play the other side of that imp and take a perverse pleasure in pushing your limits. Celebrate your victories and take pride in your accomplishments.

However, just like motivation, there are different types of pride. Not all of them are useful in strengthening our willpower. In fact, some feelings of pride can even be damaging to our goals. A study from the *Journal of Consumer Research* found that the source of our pride determines whether it will help or hinder our willpower.[16] Those who took pride in themselves were able to increase their self-control more than those who took pride in their actions.

Let's break that down: the more pride you have in your actions, the less likely you are to exercise self-control. When you take pride in eating healthy all day, you're more likely to overindulge in the evening. But when you take pride in who you are as a person— whether it's being someone who eats healthy, a daily exerciser, or a parent who always makes time for their children—you're more likely to keep up your target behavior. In short, identifying with who you *are* over what you *do* leads to greater staying power when it comes to following through on your goals.

How can we walk the fine line between pride in what we do and pride in who we are? The authors of the study recommend being in tune with your emotions, veering away from overconfidence, and remembering that it's okay to feel proud. When you take a step toward your goal, contextualize it. Use it to help define who you are. Waking up 15 minutes early isn't a good reason to sleep late the next day, but it's a great step toward your journey of being a "morning person." Each time you do it, you solidify your target identity—and that's something to be proud of.

Exercising Willpower

What exercising your willpower will look like depends on your starting point and your own particular hurdles. But wherever you start, the key is to get going and to keep pushing. If you regularly run 5K a day, continuing to do so might be easier than walking around the block every day for someone who has been sitting on their couch for the last few years.

Training your conception of your willpower is as easy (and as hard) as training any other muscle. The key is to start small, make sure that you maintain good form and use mindfulness to seek novelty in what you're doing. The root of the challenge lies within you. That's where willpower training has to occur. The most effective formula is to start where you are, build from there, and celebrate your victories as you go, taking pride in the work you are putting in and the results you are getting—both from the activities you're doing, and from the willpower effect that pushing past your limits will bring. You might be surprised at what you can accomplish when you free yourself from your own limitations.

CHAPTER 10

Willpower as a Team Sport

"Ranieri, Ranieri, he came from Italy, to manage the City."
—Leicester City football chant sung
to the tune of "Volare"

No matter how you feel about soccer (or "football" for two of the book's three authors), it's difficult to come up with a more inspiring sports team than the 2015–2016 Leicester City Football Club (Leicester City FC).

Leicester City FC, founded in the East Midlands of England in 1884, spent the majority of its existence as a lower league team. The English Football League pyramid is an interconnected hierarchy of divisions in which teams advance or decline in rank based on their performance in their division. If a team in the Premier League (the top division) fails to beat a Championship League team (the second-highest level), it can fall from the Premier League. Leicester City, sitting solidly in the second tier Championship League, was at risk of being relegated down to the Third Division in the early 1990s—but in the 1995–1996 Football League playoffs, the team managed to move up to the top league and by the 2014–2015 season, it was ranked 14th out of the top 20 Premier League teams.

In 2015, Claudio Ranieri, as the newly appointed manager of Leicester City, had put together a team of ragtag underdogs. Altogether, his starting players cost just £23 million ($29 million). The team's top opponent, Chelsea, was spending almost 10× that on their players.

Other Premier League teams, like Manchester City and Manchester United, were spending upward of £150 million ($185 million). The odds of Leicester City winning the league were pegged at 5,000 to 1.

That's when the team started to play like no other in history: not because of raw talent, but through coaching, teamwork, and camaraderie. Their unconventional style and shared desire to win outstripped what their abilities would have suggested.[1] Ranieri was known for keeping spirits high among his players, dishing out promises of pizza, and avoiding tough-guy mind games. He created an unbreakable sense of unity and willpower, pushing his players to abandon their egos, work toward a clear sense of purpose, and perhaps most importantly, to never give up. The team won or drew many of their games with late goals, outlasting their opponents. On paper, the team wasn't much in the form of talent, but that didn't stop it from beating the odds and winning the Premier League for the first time in club history. No other team has achieved an underdog win on that scale.

As Leicester City FC proved, team efforts can push us to be more than the sum of our parts. Though we often conceptualize willpower as an individual trait, groups of people can utilize a collective willpower to achieve their aims. However, group willpower differs from individual willpower. We're easily influenced by those around us: sometimes this influence isn't that positive—we're more likely to smoke cigarettes if our social circle does;[2] we're more likely to binge drink if we think our friends do it (even if they don't).[3] But sometimes it promotes prosocial behaviors—we're more likely to be environmentally conscious when those around us are.[4] We're social creatures; no one wants to be the odd one out. And that feeling extends to willpower.

Willpower as a Group Superpower

This social effect means that willpower can be at its strongest when shared by a group. Examples abound of groups that made a difficult decision and that, by deciding as a unit, overcame resistance that they would have never been able to surmount individually. In fact, intentional contagion (building on, borrowing from, or adapting the intentions of others) can help us do things we might not have thought possible by ourselves.

One of the best examples of a group overcoming an immense challenge is Sir Ernest Shackleton's voyage of 1914–1916. His ship, aptly named the *Endurance*, was trapped in the ice and crushed, forcing Shackleton and his men to survive in the Antarctic. Shackleton and five crew members braved an 800-mile journey in an open boat to a remote whaling station, then traversed the island looking for help. The crew had a clear shared objective—to survive. And despite his internal doubts and misgivings, Shackleton showed an unwavering belief that they would make it. Not only that, but he also was very clear with objectives and the role that each crew member needed to play. Their collective willpower and resilience meant that all of the 28 crew members of the *Endurance* were rescued.

We haven't all been stranded in Antarctica, but we've all experienced moments where a sense of group unity has pushed us beyond our limits. Anyone who has run a long-distance race will know the energy that comes from the support of those around you and how you can push yourself to run faster if you follow someone else. That's why they have pace setters in big races.

Experts have identified forms of willpower that only exist in a group setting—and group willpower can be far stronger than the willpower we experience individually. Based on his previous research on social-cognitive theory, Stanford professor Albert Bandura expands notions of agency beyond the personal.[5] He describes three different types of agency that humans can feel: personal, proxy, and collective. Each level increases in complexity:

- ◆ Personal: I want that apple; I reach for that apple.
- ◆ Proxy: I want that apple, so I ask you to pass it to me.
- ◆ Collective: We all want apples, so we work together to get some.

When employing collective willpower, both the goals and the work required to achieve those goals must be collective. In addition to being the most complex, collective willpower is also the most powerful. Research shows that perceived efficacy has a strong positive effect on group performance. You don't have to look further than the Leicester City story, or the heroic efforts of soldiers or first responders to see group willpower in action. Leicester FC wouldn't have made it nearly as far as it did without believing in the strength of their teammates. It was through the power of collective efficacy that the players empowered themselves to beat 5,000-to-1 odds. These effects can be seen in any group context, from team sports to scientific research to politics. So how can a group unlock collective willpower?

> Almost 90% of people believe that the willpower of a team can be stronger than the willpower of each team member.

The Three Keys to Sharing Willpower

Though a variety of factors drive willpower in a team context, there are three key ingredients to building willpower in teams. The first and most important is *a shared vision and clarity around goals.*[6] In other words, *shared intention*. When teams align on their ideal outcome and the fact that each person is needed to achieve those shared goals, they become accountable to one another. This inter-reliance drives us to outperform what we could have achieved individually. A second crucial component is *supportive leadership*—having leaders who encourage and celebrate high willpower successes.[7] The third is a set of *clear expectations with accountability for results from each contributor*.[8] Shackleton used all of these tools to great effect, communicating often with his crew about what they were collectively trying to achieve, allowing them to express themselves, supporting them even in small wins, and giving each crew member a clear role. He refused to give up, and that was evident to his team.

Not everyone on a team will have a nonlimited willpower mindset. But as long as a few key members do, the entire team can reap the benefits. Scientific research shows that willpower beliefs can have an outsized effect on a team. Individuals who push through challenges at work based on their beliefs about willpower have a positive effect on their colleagues even if they are not in official leadership positions. These nonlimited believers can, through their mindset, drive collective job performance for those around them. This effect is even stronger when a group of colleagues all believe in nonlimited willpower and act accordingly.[9] Willpower beliefs can also be contagious in a team context—one person can enhance the power of their whole team by sharing their perception of willpower as a nonlimited resource.

Closer Teams Share Willpower Better

Not surprisingly, collective willpower is dependent on the quality of the relationships among team members. As we all know from personal experience (whether at work, on a sports team or in the military), the closer the personal connections among the team members, the greater the effect of collective willpower. This doesn't mean that team members need to resemble each other. On the contrary, a significant body of research shows that more diverse teams produce better results.[10] But the more aligned the team is in terms of its willingness to go the extra mile for the collective, such as with Leicester City, the stronger the effect of the collective devotion to the goal.[11]

This isn't surprising, of course. When we know that our coworkers are as devoted and hardworking as we are, we're driven to put in the extra effort. Knowing this, the challenge for any leader (or nonleader team member) is to actively implement this effect. Anyone on a team can boost the team willpower effect by sharing and celebrating when other team members show nonlimited willpower beliefs, incentivizing the belief switch in others. This isn't about celebrating folks who work constantly and sleep in the office (or don't sleep at all!), but rather highlighting those moments when an individual or a team went beyond what was thought to be possible from them. Leadership can also create opportunities for team members to see each other overcoming seemingly intractable obstacles by sharing stories and focusing the team's attention on these moments. Leaders can also create opportunities for teams to stretch themselves in the form of Outward Bound or NOLS-like corporate retreats or charitable activities like building houses for Habitat for Humanity.

Training for Team Willpower

Training teams in willpower requires a similar approach to training willpower in individuals. Team rituals and celebrating small wins both help build momentum and instill pride in the group. Here, it is important to ensure that team members are made aware of others' victories, that they have bought into the process, and that they are also setting willpower goals for themselves. The ultimate goal is to provide team members with an opportunity to believe in themselves. Once they believe in themselves, they can start to make that magic happen on their own and reinforce it collectively.

By building a culture of nonlimited willpower belief—starting with themselves—leaders can help their teams better overcome obstacles. We won't all win the Premier League or row across the Antarctic Sea, but by borrowing tactics from those who have, we can make any team we're on a higher performing one. Simultaneously, we will be instilling a culture of engagement that will have influence throughout our organizations and even beyond the workplace.

PART III

Curiosity

CHAPTER 11

High Performers Are Curious

"Curiosity is one of the permanent and certain characteristics of a vigorous intellect."

—Samuel Johnson

Temple Grandin was born in Boston in 1947. From a young age, she was described by those around her as "different." Her parents took her to see doctors, who initially diagnosed her with "brain damage." It was only much later that she was told that she was on the autism spectrum.

At the time, her diagnosis came with a recommendation for institutionalization. While her father was ready to follow that advice, her mother didn't want her child taken away from her. While the disagreement on whether to institutionalize Grandin might have contributed to her parents' divorce, society was all the better for it. Due to an insatiable curiosity that she applied to herself and the world around her, Grandin has become an admired public figure, sticking up for the voiceless who are told that their neurodiversity makes them a burden on society.

From an early age, Grandin was profoundly interested in the ways that animals think and interact with their surroundings. While she found it hard to communicate with people, she felt at ease with animals and believed that she could understand their experience of the world. In the early 1960s in the United States, her animal-centered worldview was surprisingly new—no one in the modern agriculture industry had ever cared as deeply as Grandin did, nor had seen the world from her perspective.

Grandin's fascination led her to study animal science, eventually receiving a PhD from the University of Illinois at Urbana-Champaign. She went on to focus on the effects of fear and types of stressors on cattle, becoming one of the first scientists to promote humane alternatives to traditional livestock handling systems. Her work has had a profound effect on animal welfare. Her teachings have been embraced by animal rights activists, but also by meat producers like Cargill and global companies like McDonald's. However, Grandin's work with animals barely scratches the surface of her impact.

Challenged by her difficulty in understanding other people, Grandin wanted to figure out how she was different, and more importantly, help other people understand her. Her decision to explore her own mind and share it with the world forever changed the way people view autism. In Steve Silberman's book *NeuroTribes*, on the history of autism, the author writes that Grandin had a major impact on reducing the social stigma that previously existed around autism.[1] As research psychologist Bernarn Rimland explains, "Temple's ability to convey to the reader her innermost feelings and fears, coupled with her capacity for explaining mental processes will give the reader an insight into autism that very few have been able to achieve."[2]

Grandin is a testament to the power of curiosity. Her readiness to dive into her passions and share them with the world led to a more humane and understanding society.

Knowledge for Its Own Sake

Curiosity is a foundational building block of intention: it's the engine that hums along, driving all the other ingredients forward. Make someone curious enough, and they'll be able to recruit the willpower, attention, integrity, and habits they need to satisfy that curiosity.

The curiosity that drove Grandin is a critical ingredient to high performance. Fortunately, most of us have already experienced what it's like to be good at being curious, and the fact that you're reading this book shows that you have a measure of curiosity. Or, more accurately, a sign that you haven't yet lost all of your wonder at the magic of the world. As children, we're naturally inclined to explore and discover. We had little worry about how others might perceive us or the outcomes of our discoveries. We used to be curious for the sake of it. We may still be pretty good at being curious, but as children, we were great at it.

Curiosity is generally understood in psychology as seeking out knowledge for its own sake, instead of for its utility.[3] As a child, you might have tried the potion of dirt and water you made just to see what it tasted like. As a child, Grandin might have followed a cat around just to see how it behaved—not to inform the 60+ academic papers on animal behavior she would later write. Curiosity pushes us to explore the world without bogging ourselves down in what we might be able to get out of it. Like the Langerian mindfulness previously explored, curiosity is about seeking out what we haven't seen before, what is novel—just to be present with it.

But just because curiosity isn't focused on outcomes doesn't mean there aren't tangible benefits to being curious. Curiosity, for instance, pushes us to retain information, which can help us be better learners. In two similar studies, participants were asked trivia questions about a wide range of subjects, rating their level of curiosity to find out the answer for each.[4,5] Unsurprisingly, the participants—both young and old—were better at remembering trivia that piqued their curiosity. But it wasn't just the trivia that they remembered better. In between rounds of questions, they were shown images of faces, entirely unrelated to the trivia. The researchers found that the faces that were shown close in time to the high-curiosity trivia questions were also more easily remembered by participants. In other words, being in a curious state of mind may make us more receptive, even to topics outside of the current focus of our curiosity.

And the tangible benefits don't stop there. Curiosity leads to a breadth of other positive outcomes, including improved academic performance,[6] increased well-being,[7] lower cognitive decline in older adults,[8] and a stronger sense of meaningfulness in goals and day-to-day life.[9] We're even more likely to see better outcomes at work when employees are driven by curiosity. Curiosity has been established as a significant predictor of job performance, especially compared to other more traditional personality traits used to assess employees like extraversion, agreeableness, and conscientiousness.[10]

Curiosity even explains some of the divergence in work performance that can't be explained by more traditional personality traits. For example, it is unlikely that you've ever heard of Percy Spencer, but we'd be willing to bet that you use the product of his curiosity at least once a day. During the Second World War, Spencer was an engineer working for a U.S. Department of Defense contractor building radar tubes, and he was awarded the U.S. Navy's distinguished service award for that work. But one day, while working on powerful vacuum tubes to be used in radar systems, he noticed that the candy bar in his pocket melted. Rather than ascribing the melted candy bar to the heat from his leg, or ignoring it so he could get his work done, Spencer got curious and investigated. Figuring that the machine he was working on had somehow heated the candy bar, he experimented with other foods and realized that electromagnetic fields can produce heat. He tried this out with corn kernels that popped when placed close to the machines, and the microwave oven was born. Many of today's modern unicorn tech firms have grown out of similar stories of people seeing something strange happening and deciding to investigate further, seeing if they can find a way to solve a problem that no one else had articulated before.

The Real Superpower: Focused Curiosity

To make the leap between general curiosity and productive investigation, you need focus. As investor Paul Graham said in his famous "Bus Ticket Collector" essay: "Everyone knows that to do great work you need both natural ability and determination. But there's a third ingredient that's not as well understood: an obsessive interest in a particular topic."[11] Note that it's not knowledge he's referring to here, but *interest*. You have to be insanely curious. When that's assigned to a particular topic, that's where great things happen. All important scientific discoveries came as a result of someone focusing intently on a particular problem for years or even decades. Turning it over in their minds until they unlocked the answer. We'll talk more about focus in Chapter 20, as it's a crucial ingredient in turning curiosity into an intentional superpower, but for now, let's look at why we don't value curiosity more and how we can build our curiosity back up.

85% of people believe that curiosity is a driving force of high performance.

Living the Atelic Life

Many of us learned as kids that asking too many questions isn't always rewarded. Our frazzled parents didn't usually have time to explain to us why the sky is blue as they packed our lunch and sent us off to school. It takes effort to de-program ourselves out of the lessons learned as we entered adulthood. Many of us long ago forgot the joys of small, utility-free endeavors. As we age, more and more of our actions are determined by obligation or gain, instead of sheer, uninhibited interest.

Though some personality traits (like our conscientiousness) increase as we age, our openness decreases.[12] Even though curiosity is a "fundamental part of human motivation,"[13] adults just don't have the same interest in the world beyond their bubble that kids do. Specifically, we see a decline in three particular types of curiosity as we age: interpersonal (caring about other people), intrapersonal (caring about ourselves) and epistemic curiosity (our basic desire for new knowledge).[4]

It can be disheartening to envision our ability to be curious—and all the benefits that accompany it—declining as we age. But there are practices we can adopt to reverse this trend. If we want to reap the benefits of this superpower, we should adopt atelic activities as part of our everyday lives.

Atelic? Blame Aristotle, who differentiated between two types of pursuits: telic and atelic. Telic (from the Greek *telos* meaning "end" or "goal") are activities that have a purpose. Atelic activities are done without a clear goal in mind—more focused on the process than the outcome.

To explore this topic further, we spoke with Dr. Kieran Setiya, a philosophy professor from MIT who promotes participation in atelic activities in *Midlife: A Philosophical Guide*, his book on navigating middle age through the teachings of philosophy. In our conversation, he discussed how as we grow, and especially in early to mid-adulthood, we become more focused on telic activities, causing us to be less naturally curious and more focused on doing for the sake of achievement.[14]

In his book, Setiya explains that we overweight telic activities so much that many of us see no need for activities that don't have explicit utility. We practice the piano in order to please our mother-in-law or slow cognitive decline, not just to do it. We read a book in order to check it off our list and gain new knowledge for the workplace. We go for a walk in nature because we think it'll be good for us, not just to enjoy the walking itself, or "finding value in the process of what we are doing in a way that makes the present seem fuller, more satisfying—and more apt for attention and engagement."[15] To counteract this, we can endeavor to spend more time traveling to new places, reading books on subjects that we know nothing about (that are unrelated to our jobs), and seeking out new experiences: trying novel things not because we want to achieve something, but rather to be present in the moment with those activities. And that is the true meaning of engagement—being present in what you are doing.

> As a short thought experiment, ask yourself what you would do if you had a free day where you could do anything you wanted, but with one condition—what you do cannot be in service to some other goal. That is, you're not allowed to go for a run if you're running to get into shape, or prepare for a marathon, or even just to clear your head. What would you do just to do that thing?

For many of us, this is a surprisingly difficult question to answer. We're so caught up with telic activities that we've forgotten how to do things that have no purpose outside of themselves.

Of course, it's not always realistic to put aside time for meandering. Most of us have busy lives; a large part of our lack of pointless hobbies is simply that we have too much on our plates. Setiya acknowledges that sometimes the demands of life are too pressing to engage in regular atelic activities. But the shift from telic to atelic doesn't have to mean a shift in activity. It can be a shift in mindset.

"Most of the things you'll be doing at any given time will be describable in both ways," Setiya explains. "You don't necessarily need to shift what you're doing, but just try to find the atelic in it, and find the value in that. I'm not going to stop writing philosophy articles, but the point is to be doing philosophy, not just to get the article done."[16]

If you don't have time to spend on new experiences (though we highly recommend trying to find some if you can), try reframing. The next time you cook dinner, break out of the obligation of the task. Sure, you have to feed yourself, but look for some intrinsic enjoyment in it. Do you love experimenting with spice blends? Trying dishes from countries you've never been to? Perfecting your Tex-Mex taco? Be playful and curious for no reason other than to enjoy the moment—for nothing in return. As Setiya told us, shifting his mindset in this way about his work helped him navigate his way through his own version of a midlife crisis. "The shift to a more atelic mindset changed my life: it made the present seem less empty, less of a frustrating rat race or hamster wheel and put me back in touch with what I really valued."[17]

Curiosity—the ability to wonder and question—calcifies as we age and we build a set of beliefs about the way the world is and should be. In the following chapters, we discuss how fighting against this tendency and keeping our curiosity flexible is so important in the context of intention.

CHAPTER 12

Don't Stop (Re)believing

"In all affairs, it's a healthy thing now and then to hang a question mark on the things you have long taken for granted."

—Bertrand Russell

Picture this: you embark on a three-day hike through pristine, untouched wilderness. You have a basic map of the terrain and a plan for each day. You set off, following the map as precisely as you can, though you get a bit distracted by the beauty of the landscape. A few hours into your hike, you notice a small hill due north of you. You recognize the hill on your map, and you feel confident you're on the right path. A few hours pass, and you start to get tired. Your campsite should be just a mile or two away. As you continue forward, the sun now casting long shadows, you hear running water ahead. The noise grows louder and louder, until you finally find yourself standing at the edge of a roaring river, blocking your path. As tiny droplets spray your face, your pulse quickens and you realize something. This river is not on the map. At least not on the part of the map where you thought you were.

What would you do in this situation? Would you a) embrace the idea that you've perhaps misread the map, or b) assume that the river isn't really there and continue walking forward?

As ridiculous as this example sounds, studies on cognitive biases like confirmation bias, cognitive dissonance, and belief perseverance show that people have a surprisingly hard time revising their beliefs when faced with new evidence. Instead, people exhibit *motivated reasoning*—using biased logic and reasoning to double down on their beliefs. For example, showing climate change deniers evidence of climate change makes them . . . somehow believe even less in climate change.[1] Surprisingly, this form of inflexible thinking doesn't seem to be the result of rushing to conclusions, intuiting things or using a set of mental shortcuts. As Dan Kahan at Yale Law School has shown, motivated reasoning is actually associated with higher degrees of cognitive reflection.[2]

People who exhibit more motivated reasoning (and we all exhibit some) tend to think more and harder about the issue at hand. Motivated reasoning isn't a sign of stupidity, as the conventional wisdom might have you believe. It's a feature of our brain's ability to process information, pushing us to interpret evidence in a way that serves our interests (rather than the interest of some objective truth). Whether those interests are a sense of belonging to a group (or even the notion that we're great hikers), the result is a set of beliefs that don't match the reality around us. As Kahan points out, this is often the rational thing to do from a personal self-identity perspective. Would you rather be right and ostracized from your community, or wrong but well integrated? The problem, as we all know, arises when a large group of people collectively find shelter in a valley of incorrect (although convenient) truths. But that's a story for another book.

The Art of Changing Your Mind

Paul, a close friend of Mike's and a wildly successful stock trader, likes to say: "In trading, strong beliefs are like booster rockets— useful to get you close, but you want to discard them as quickly as you can, since they'll only hold you back." Another way to express this comes from Stanford Professor and futurist Paul Saffo who favors: "strong opinions, weakly held."

This approach, which is also the foundation of the McKinsey problem-solving method, encourages you to start with a hypothesis, even if all the information isn't yet known (as can happen in new industries or with challenging problems). But the most important part is that, as new information is uncovered, you have to be able to change your hypotheses. Present your idea, but be prepared to change it.

Skilled critical thinkers aren't only able to change their mind, they're able to entertain different points of view at the same time. They constantly reassess what they believe, seeking new information, and in the right circumstances, integrate opposing viewpoints into their mental models to create novel approaches. Morgan Housel, the author of *The Psychology of Money*, calls this "mental liquidity" and argues that in the context of investing, the ability to change your mind is under-valued: "So much of what people call "conviction" is actually a willful disregard for facts that might change their minds. It's dangerous because conviction feels like a good attribute, while its opposite—being wishy-washy—makes you feel and sound like an idiot."[3]

How to Get Cognitively Flexible

Researchers have long studied how we adjust our beliefs, referred to as *cognitive flexibility*. There's two different types of beliefs here: there are Beliefs (big-*B*, such as a belief in democracy or dignity for all individuals) and beliefs (small-*b*, such as a belief that a puzzle piece fits just there, that wombats are marsupials, or that New York City is in the United States). And it is in the context of small-*b* beliefs that cognitive flexibility is a crucial skill.

We are all familiar with this ability, which, grounded in curiosity, allows us to practice "belief adjustment" or "mind changing" in a tactical way as we go about our day. We were confident that the puzzle piece would fit right there on the left side, but oops, it actually goes over here on the top right. *Cognitive flexibility* can be roughly defined as doing something one way, discovering that it doesn't work, and doing it another way. Allanny Nunes de Santana and colleagues carried out a meta-analysis[4] that found a strong correlation between cognitive flexibility and math performance. Cognitive flexibility has also been found to predict better reading skills,[5] Sudoku performance,[6] and yes, even life satisfaction.[7] Unsurprisingly perhaps, being able to admit that our current strategy is failing is a strong predictor of eventually succeeding.

To build this skill, think of a small-*b* belief you've held for a long time—something fairly innocuous, but that is important to you. Assess the strength of your belief on a scale of 1–10. Now, at the risk of losing you down an internet rabbit hole, spend a little while trying to prove yourself and your belief wrong (this might take 15 minutes or maybe even a few hours). Actively go out and search for evidence that contradicts your belief and try to find perspectives other than your own. Be fair and open here—imagine that you were someone who believed the opposite and seek evidence to support your newfound perspective. Really subject this belief to a reality check: actively search for evidence that contradicts your belief and for alternative perspectives that challenge it. At the end of the exercise, ask yourself, how strongly do you now believe in your original position? Has that changed? If not, can you at least see a little more clearly why others might believe the other side of the argument?

But what about stubbornness or stick-to-it-iveness? Interestingly, in one study on cognitive flexibility, Vrinda Kalia and colleagues found that grit (a form of perseverance and resilience) and cognitive flexibility have to go hand in hand to result in high performance. Those who persevere without changing strategies, simply trying to brute force their way, don't do very well. Similarly, those who adapt their strategy but quickly give up don't cut it. It's only by combining the ability to keep trying with a certain detachment from past approaches that the researchers saw the best performers shine through.

The Science of Cognitive Flexibility

The idea that cognitive flexibility is a trainable skill isn't just wishful thinking. In a 2018 study,[8] Cristine Legare and her colleagues at the University of Texas, Austin wanted to determine how learnable cognitive flexibility really is. Is it something immutable or something trainable? Are we born with cognitive flexibility, or can we improve it?

To sort this out, they compared three- to five-year-olds from America with their counterparts in South Africa. They wanted to see to what extent cognitive flexibility would vary between countries. After giving the kids language tests, they found that while other learning measures seemed to be fairly consistent across these cultures, cognitive flexibility varied significantly (with the American kids scoring higher than their South African counterparts). They concluded that while other traits may be more "fixed," cognitive flexibility is somehow culturally imparted; it's something we're taught—and can teach ourselves.

Through a variety of interventions (computerized training, games, aerobics, martial arts, yoga, mindfulness, and school curricula), the authors in *Science* showed that cognitive flexibility can be trained in 4–12 year olds.[9] And other research suggests that there is hope for adults too.[10] In an experiment, scientists provided executive control (the ability to use complex mental processes to carry out goal-directed behavior) training to participants of three age groups: 8–10, 18–26, and 62–76 year olds. They found that, across all three groups, cognitive flexibility can be trained and significantly improved. Task-switching training (moving between tasks) can help people of all ages improve their cognitive flexibility scores. The effect was strongest in children and older adults, though it was still present in the 18–26 year olds. And the secret to doing this lies in curiosity. We need to be able to keep our minds open and seek out new information. Yes, we were convinced that we read the map right, but now we've discovered that we were wrong. Rather than trying to convince ourselves that we're still right, or argue with the facts that we see before us, we need to open our minds and process our discovery and find a new path. And so, the ability to revise small-*b* beliefs seems to be a matter of curiosity and practice. But what about big-*B* Beliefs? That deserves its own chapter, coming up next.

CHAPTER 13

How to Change Your Mind

"We don't see things as they are, we see them as we are."

—Anaïs Nin

Small-*b* beliefs—the small, tactical beliefs that we form throughout the day—can be disheartening to change but aren't all that difficult to adjust. You thought the answer to 13 across in this week's *New Yorker* crossword (clue: "beaming") was "SHINE," but oops, it seems like it was "SMILE." Small-*b* beliefs exist in the tactical realm where training cognitive flexibility with curiosity can help us be better at navigating daily life. However, as we move toward big-*B* Beliefs, a different story unfolds.

Big-*B* Beliefs are. . .well, bigger. They're the lenses we use to approach big issues, the attitudes that help us make sense of the world around us. What is the meaning of life? Are we alone in the universe? Should we eat animals? Big-*B* Beliefs are the tools we use to proclaim our moral, social, or political stance to the world. Since they serve all of these roles, they feel like a core part of our identity. But that doesn't mean they're always accurate or even self-serving.

The ability to re-evaluate big-*B* Beliefs is a difficult but critical part of intention. It allows us to integrate new evidence into our worldviews. Take the Belief that "boiling lobsters alive is okay" as an example. Oops, a new study shows that lobsters can feel pain (or we just read *Consider the Lobster* by David Foster Wallace). Boiling lobsters alive is now not okay. This seems easy enough if you don't

95

have strong opinions about lobsters. But replace "boiling lobsters alive" with the most recent political issue that made you fume, and you'll start to see the immense challenge in changing our minds.

Revising big-*B* Beliefs can feel like an affront to our character. If lobster boils are steeped into our culture, we might not be at all open to the latest research on their pain receptors. Instead of rationally integrating new evidence into our Beliefs, we might turn to dismissal or anger. Lobster eaters in New Brunswick or Maine might not just love lobster boils—lobster boils may be part of who they feel they are. It may be natural for them to deprioritize the concerns of animal rights activists who want to put the interests of lobsters over preserving a traditional cooking culture. And on the other side, it's natural for activists who picket for lobster rights to consider their opponents selfish and mean-spirited. Whichever side we fall on, we're inclined to use our Beliefs to protect and define our identities. And this is a point we need to consider or at least question: to what degree do our Beliefs really shape our identities? And are we confident that all of our big-*B* Beliefs are actually helping us?

The more powerful or deeply held our Belief is, the less likely we are to engage in reasonable discussion, and the more likely we are to be reactive to opposing views. This is painfully visible all around us. Governments often try to use rational information to change big-*B* Beliefs and wind up confused and dismayed when a large part of their target audience digs their heels in deeper as if they don't care about the truth.[1] The reality is that deeply ingrained Beliefs are notoriously difficult to tackle. But the ability to face them, both in ourselves and in others, is key to building a more intentional life.

Techniques to Reduce Extreme Beliefs

Despite their gargantuan challenge, there are plenty of groups working to change the way that we address big-*B* Beliefs in others. The Institute for Strategic Dialogue (ISD) is a nonprofit that aims to reverse polarization, extremism, and disinformation around the world. And it is not alone. Organizations like the Counter Extremism Project, Los Angeles LGBT Center, and the Deep Canvass Institute, among others, are all working alongside the ISD to better our Belief systems and approaches. Given the large-scale problems that face our planet and society, the ability to navigate Beliefs cooperatively is arguably one of the most important challenges we currently face.

Two-thirds of people admit to feeling a strong emotional reaction when their Beliefs are challenged.

At the heart of this challenge is that when pushed to change or even question our Beliefs, we can feel alienated or "othered," entrenching us even further in those Belief systems. Instead of adding to the problem and creating deeper divides, these organizations have based their influence techniques in behavioral science, such as a well-proven approach called *deep canvassing*.

Deep canvassing originated at the Los Angeles LGBT Center in 2012 after staff started a dialogue with Californians to understand why they had voted against same-sex marriage. Deep canvassing focuses on creating empathic conversations, active listening, and sharing personal stories to form genuine connections. The goal isn't to peddle an opinion or force a new conclusion. The goal is to encourage reflection. While early evidence was mixed (including an early study with falsified data that destroyed its reputation), more recent data has supported the efficacy of deep canvassing.[2] Non-persuasive but emotionally connected conversations can help soften, and even reverse, extreme Beliefs. Deep canvassing is effective, but only when canvassers are nonjudgmental in their discussions.[3] In 2020, two political scientists from Yale and University of California, Berkeley sent 230 canvassers to knock on doors in seven U.S. cities. Each canvasser had the intention of discussing divisive issues with Americans—like immigration policy and transphobia—to reduce prejudiced beliefs.

Across 6,869 conversations, they found that arguments for voters to reconsider hot topics did little to change their minds. But the political scientists also found that a nonjudgmental conversation, a simple exchange of narratives, could reduce prejudiced beliefs. In fact, the strategy was still working when the researchers checked back four months later. It appears that we don't want to be told to change our minds. But most of us are open to learning more about other people, especially if we feel any kind of affinity to them. This includes being open to learning how other people think, which helps us reflect on how we think.

While there are many books out there on how to change other people's minds (our favorite is *How Minds Change* by David McRaney—where he goes into far more detail on deep canvassing and related techniques), we're interested in whether these techniques can be applied to changing our own minds—a necessity in the context of living an intentional life.

Deep Canvassing Inward

There are plenty of resources on how to change someone else's mind. We'd all love to convince our aunt that a microwave won't give her cancer or help our neighbor understand that astronauts walking on the moon wasn't staged. But there aren't as many of us who passionately want to change our *own* beliefs (especially our big-*B* Beliefs)—or even critically examine them. For those who do want to take a closer look at their Beliefs, however, the same techniques that can change other people's minds can be applied to our own.

The place to start is with the understanding that humans are social animals. We evolved to believe what those around us believe. Since we depend on those around us for safety and belonging, veering away from our accepted social norms is, from an evolutionary perspective, dangerous.[4] We depend on our community for survival, and for much of our human history being ostracized from our community was tantamount to a death sentence. At the same time, inheriting Beliefs by virtue of belonging to a certain group can drive us toward unintentional and inauthentic lives—something that has the potential for personal and societal alienation. But there's no need to burn it all to the ground. We can start by understanding how some of our core Beliefs arose in the first place.

Dig down to the core of one of your Beliefs. Don't start with your deepest-held values. Start broad. Instead of your most-impassioned political values, start with a Belief you'd be open to a conversation about. A few potential examples: is it okay to eat animals? Are we alone in the universe? Are humans inherently good? Will AI make the world a better place? Define your stance and then ask yourself a few questions about that Belief:

◆ Was there ever a time you didn't believe it?
◆ Do the people close to you hold this Belief?
◆ How are people who don't share this Belief different from you?
◆ How does the process that led them to their Belief differ from the one that led you to yours?
◆ What would it take to change your mind about it?

Asking these questions can feel uncomfortable, but they're useful tools to help you understand your own thought processes. If you can get in the habit of investigating your Beliefs, you'll be able to better connect with opposing views in the future. Perhaps you'll even integrate pieces of opposing views into your own Belief systems. But don't worry: The point of the exercise isn't to brainwash yourself. It's simply a practice in nuanced thinking as a step on the path toward living a more intentional life. To continue this exercise, seek out others who feel differently about an issue than you do—not to try to convince them, but to understand the roots of their convictions, and in so doing to better understand the roots of your own. Ask questions of them, and while you're doing so, welcome their questions of you.

As you follow this Belief exploration process, you're also likely to encounter the emotions tied to your Beliefs. It's the emotive nature of big-*B* Beliefs that makes them so profound and techniques like deep canvassing so effective. Conversations are built from an emotional connection. Therefore, as you start to understand how a core Belief was born, think about the emotional aspects of that Belief. What are the emotional needs that the Belief is serving (such as belonging, safety, connection)? Is it serving these needs well? Do you think that people who have a very different Belief on this topic have different emotional needs? What might happen to your emotions if this Belief were to change? The prospect of a Belief changing, together with what that may mean for us emotionally, brings us to the next part—questioning the consequences.

What Do You Get from Your Beliefs?

While there are many philosophical perspectives on what makes a "good" Belief, the extent to which the Belief correctly represents the world is certainly a central ingredient. But humans aren't insensitive truth machines, nor should we strive to be. The truth can be useful, like the small-*b* belief of knowing whether or not there's a hidden patch of ice on your double black diamond ski hill. But there are times when it isn't the best option—like letting your mother-in-law know what you really think of her eggplant curry. So assessing our own Beliefs should include taking stock of what we're getting out of them, how they are in some way supporting a sense of self or identity and how they fulfill an emotional need.

Take your chosen big-*B* Belief from the earlier exercise and ask yourself a couple more questions: what are the consequences of believing this? What might be the consequences of believing something else? If the consequences of a Belief can cause harm to yourself or others, it's worth investing time into reassessment. And we might also extend our notion of harm to include the absence of something good, not just the presence of something negative. For example, the Belief that small children should not be comforted when they are upset so that they learn to be strong could be harmful—even though those who believe this are arguably not actively causing harm and probably big-*B* Believe that they are doing the right thing for their children.

Changing Beliefs in others is hard—doubly so in one's self. However, this is a journey worth embarking on. By developing a more nuanced and more complete understanding of our world—and our internal world in particular—we can break down barriers and approach our challenges and goals with openness rather than hostility. As a closing thought on this invitation to get to know yourself better and more authentically, remember that re-evaluating your Beliefs is not about ridding yourself of "wrong thoughts." It's about starting an ongoing dialogue with yourself, with your community, and with the world you inhabit. It's a dialogue rooted in curiosity, empathy, and a willingness to grow beyond the result of a set of circumstances. In other words, it is to truly be intentional.

CHAPTER 14

Believing Together

"Whenever you find yourself on the side of the majority, it is time to pause and reflect."

—Mark Twain

In one of the most famous psychology experiments of all time, Solomon Asch showed a group of participants some sets of lines.[1] Each member of the group, in turn, would declare which line was the same length as a target line.

Try it for yourself with the following example.[2] Which of the three lines matches the target line on the left?

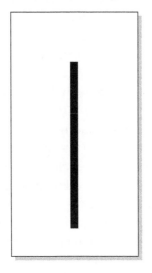 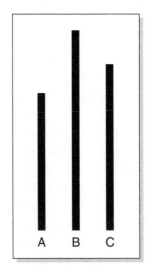

Pretty easy, right? However, each experiment group contained only one real participant. The rest were confederates—actors who were paid to act as participants. Asch would begin by asking the actors which line they thought was most accurate, leaving the real participant to answer last. In the control condition (without the lying actors), there was an error rate of less than 1%. Nearly everyone could tell which lines were the same length. But when confederates were instructed to give obviously incorrect answers, real participants went along with the wider group's belief a shocking 37% of the time—even when it was painfully untrue (go back and look at those lines again!). More than 70 years later, Asch's words still ring true: "That intelligent, well-meaning, young people are willing to call white black is a matter of concern."[3] If you've ever bitten your tongue rather than express a contrary opinion to the way that a group wanted to go, you've witnessed this for yourself. We were easily swayed by our peers 60 years ago, and we're easily swayed by our peers now.

Two Minds Aren't Always Better than One

In 2010, researchers from the Interacting Minds Project at Aarhus University set out to find whether combining minds with someone else is better or worse than going at it solo.[4] Just like Asch's line experiment, they used a perceptual decision task, asking participants to visually discern the correct answer. Based on their eyesight, participants had different levels of success at getting the right answer—some got it right every time; others struggled.

When they paired participants together, the researchers expected them to perform at the level of the individual with the better eyesight: that a pair that contained an individual with 20/20 eyesight would give 20/20 responses. Interestingly, when pairs had similar levels of ability the group out-performed individuals (two people of similar levels would actually work together to make each other better), but when someone with great eyesight was matched with someone with poor eyesight, their combined performance would falter. The participation of an individual with poor eyesight would negatively impact the final result, despite their partner having perfect eyesight.

Why did those with perfect eyesight do worse when grouped with someone with worse eyesight? It's because groups aren't always more than the sum of their parts—especially when there are large differences in ability. When Bahrami discussed this with us, he emphasized that this is especially true when there is no outside reference and we are comparing perceptions of things—like two referees in an amateur soccer game or doctors looking at an X-ray. In these situations, we are more prone to being influenced by the less able in the group. And so, we should be especially wary in situations like this, where important decisions are being made by groups of people with varying degrees of knowledge and expertise (such as on company boards).[5]

Group Beliefs: A Whole New Ballgame

When humans find themselves in group settings, those groups become home to emergent properties: qualities that arise from the complex dynamics of a system. A simple example of an emergent property is the pattern of birds when they fly in a flock. While individual birds may fly in a fairly straightforward manner, after a flock reaches a certain size, the flock exhibits behaviors that can't be explained by examining any individual member.

The same, it turns out, holds true for beliefs. While we may envision an organization as a group of individuals, group beliefs aren't all that different from how a flock of birds fly. Group beliefs are as much a result of relationships and the system itself as they are of the members involved.

Groups of people have all kinds of idiosyncrasies. If you've ever completed a group project at school, you're likely familiar with social loafing, our tendency to give less effort in a group context than we would individually. In larger society, groups give rise to tragedies of the commons, wherein a lack of coordination depletes shared resources (think of individual farmers in an arid area overusing an aquifer or river). And at the office, we're all prone to groupthink—reaching a subpar consensus so as not to upset others.

It's not that shared beliefs are all bad. It's only in groups of people that we can partake in family traditions, or the collective hope that this year (finally!) the Montreal Canadiens hockey team is going to win the Stanley Cup again. But the power of shared beliefs has a dangerous side to it. We don't have to look much further than the political polarization and extremist beliefs of modern discourse. In extreme circumstances, group beliefs are what can lead otherwise-rational individuals to join cults or commit horrendous acts of violence. Unfortunately, our collective superpower of shared intention isn't always used for good; it's easy to get swept up in mass fear, anxiety, or misinformation.

Poor group belief hygiene is one of the biggest problems we face as a society today—it leads to wrong actions and also a lack of action when it is sorely needed. Too often we seem powerless against collective belief structures, especially once we sink into online echo chambers. Luckily, there are strategies to prevent ourselves from succumbing too far to the beliefs of others and develop better belief hygiene as groups, just like we can as individuals. But before going into how to achieve this, let's take a look at how groupthinking works.

> Nearly half of people feel conscious pressure to conform to majority opinions, even when they disagree.

Groupthinking Our Way to Disaster

Why does our decision-making falter when we're in groups? When humans get together, we're prone to all kinds of dynamics, such as social hierarchies and a need for a sense of belonging. Often, our desire to please or fit in with others leads us to make poorer decisions than we might have otherwise.

The concept of groupthink has been around since the 1950s, but it was popularized in the 1970s by Yale researcher Irving Janis. He used groupthink to explain disasters like the poor preparation in advance of the Japanese attack on Pearl Harbor and the disastrous Bay of Pigs invasion.[6] As Janis explains, groupthink is "a mode of thinking that people engage in when they are deeply involved in a cohesive in-group, when the members' strivings for unanimity override their motivation to realistically appraise alternative courses of action."[7] When we engage in groupthink, we lose out on mental clarity and moral judgment due to the pressures of aligning with the collective. This kind of thinking can occur when we feel pressure to conform to a group opinion, when a group is overly cohesive, or when members collectively construct rationales to defend their decisions.

The consequences of groupthink-ridden work environments extend far beyond sending out a mediocre client deliverable or firing the wrong person. As Janis pointed out in his seminal research, many global tragedies and disasters could have been prevented with cultures of robust dissent. One such example is NASA's 1986 *Challenger* explosion.

The *Challenger*'s infamous explosion, and the seven lives lost as a consequence, was largely due to a leak in one of its rocket boosters.[8] Investigations afterward identified thick, black smoke arising from the booster in question while still on the launch pad. The source of the leak was a small, flexible rubber ring that sealed the rocket boosters: the O-ring. The O-ring was known to lose its elasticity in cold temperatures.

Potential risks of launching on a cold, 36-degree morning—17 degrees below the O-ring's minimum temperature to function—were absent in the high-level decision-makers' choice to launch. But they weren't absent on the ground. A press conference held 12 hours before the *Challenger*'s take-off noted the low temperature and the risk of O-ring malfunction. Morning inspections found icicles formed on the launch pad, their potential consequences unknown. Key decision-makers didn't ignore these warning signs. They were never told of them. There was no information about the risky O-ring in any flight-readiness documents.

The Rogers Commission, led by former Secretary of State William P. Rogers to investigate the cause of the fatal launch, found a series of technical and communication problems, like the O-ring risks, leading up to the disaster. Their official conclusion wasn't that the cause was technical in nature. It was that NASA's decision-making process was flawed.[9] Despite the number of NASA employees who were aware of the risks, the information never made it to the top— NASA demonstrated a culture dangerously in thrall of groupthink, where no one was ready to raise a flag and properly question decisions that were already made.

So how does this happen? David Lochbaum, a nuclear engineer and former director of the Nuclear Safety Project for the Union of

Concerned Scientists, has investigated nuclear disasters that arose due to organizational failures. As he explained in an interview with the *New York Times*, "As you go up the chain, you're generally asked harder and harder questions by people who have more and more control over your future."[10] It's typical for groups to feel pressure to conform into giving a unified answer when faced with authority—small doubts are easily traded for an appearance of cohesion and competence.

Most of the organizations that we've worked with over the years exhibit similar signs of groupthink throughout their collective decision-making processes. While the stakes aren't usually as high as rocket launches, the results for companies can be extremely harmful. Well-meaning but misguided leaders tend to reward conformity and success, and often bypass or suppress intentional dissent.

Even those who claim they want to hear dissent aren't always ready to deal with its consequences. Sure, a dissenter might save the company from ruin. But most of the time, dissent doesn't lead to anything. Janis himself pointed out that the downsides of fighting groupthink can include "prolonged and costly debates when a rapidly growing crisis requires immediate solution."[11] But leaders need to be ready to accept those who go against the grain, even when they don't gain anything in the short-term. How? By creating safe, accepting environments for their employees to do so and by using tools to counteract the effects of groupthink.

Psychological Safety 101

One of the hottest topics in human resources today is psychological safety. And for good reason—it empowers us to better do our jobs. In psychologically safe environments, employees don't fear backlash for sharing ideas that go against the collective view. There's no worry that speaking up to correct your manager's mistake in an internal presentation will end with discipline or side-eyed looks from your colleagues.

Amy Edmondson is a professor at Harvard Business School and known as the leader of the psychological safety movement. She explains that the power of psychological safety comes from "a shared belief held by members of a team that the team is safe for interpersonal risk taking."[12] In a culture that successfully upholds this belief, true perspectives are never watered down due to a perceived risk of reputational damage. To create whole organizations that are psychologically safe, leaders need to diminish the risk that individuals might feel in these scenarios. As Edmondson suggested to us by email—it is also important to not make psychological safety the primary goal.[13] Essentially, psychological safety must always be in service to the defined objectives of the group (or as we would term it, the group's shared intentions)—it's a means to an end, not the end in and of itself.

Some ingredients in offsetting groupthink are naming it, encouraging dissent, conducting post- and pre-mortems, and using devil's advocates.

NAME IT

As just stated, an important step in overcoming groupthink is naming it. Every member of an organization should be aware of both the danger and the ubiquitous nature of groupthink. This step is an easy one: organizational leaders can distribute educational materials, like Janis's original works on the subject, or Amy Edmondson's book on psychological safety, *The Fearless Organization*.[14] To ensure this information doesn't go in one ear and out the other, these materials should be revisited annually or—even better—openly discussed and modeled by leadership teams.

ENCOURAGE DISSENT

To combat group decision-making, employees must feel welcome to go against the grain—even if they don't save the company each time they do it. When Mike worked at McKinsey & Company, one of the central stated values of the firm was what they called The Obligation to Dissent. The idea was that no matter where you stood in the organizational hierarchy, you had an obligation to raise your hand and dissent if you believed that a particular decision was wrong. Yet even with a standing rule, speaking out against popular opinion can be difficult and dangerous. Leaders and colleagues can encourage this behavior by thanking and celebrating employees for their efforts to dissent, even—or especially—when it doesn't lead to anything at all.

CONDUCT POST- AND PRE-MORTEMS

While learning about examples of groupthink through the Bay of Pigs invasion and other famous cases can be helpful, more applicable and relatable case studies can be found in past organizational decisions. Take a decision made not too long ago within your organization and—without ego—dissect the steps of the decision-making process. Who contributed? How quickly was an outcome reached? Did participants dissent, and if they did, were their queries meaningfully acknowledged? This activity is especially valuable when looking at past mistakes—though be vigilant that the process doesn't focus on blame. The purpose is to examine the internal social structures that led to an undesirable outcome, not to find fault in any one individual.

In the military, they use a similar tool called an after-action review (AAR) where processes, decisions, and consequences are reviewed soon after an engagement. Regular AARs can help troops avoid repeating mistakes. And the key to successfully implementing learnings from an AAR is to not just name improvements but embed them into processes. Would the decision to appoint an acting CFO last year have gone better if more employees were privy to the process? If so, make a concrete plan to increase transparency in future leadership decisions.

You can also prevent costly errors by conducting pre-mortems. Project yourself into the future, assume that the project was a complete failure and ask your team to debate potential reasons why. Looking forward, instead of behind, can take egos out of the equation. There's no blame for an event that hasn't happened!

DESIGNATE DEVIL'S ADVOCATES

We often conflate the idea of a devil's advocate with that annoying newbie student at the front of the lecture hall who thinks that they know better than everyone else. But when implemented intentionally, devil's advocacy can be a strategic tool to tackle groupthink. All it takes is appointing one decision-maker, or even a subgroup (sometimes referred to as red-teaming), to attack the decision in play. If everyone is in agreement on a decision, explicitly tasking someone with dissenting can push the team's decision-making to examine the flaws that might have been glossed over for the sake of group cohesiveness. Just be careful to not always assign this role to the same person. No one wants the reputation of a perennial devil's advocate!

Regardless of how you do it, actively fighting groupthink is crucial in organizational decision-making processes. Our minds, when thinking in tandem, are prone to all sorts of unhelpful biases. By emphasizing the harm of groupthink in an organization, leadership can help ensure that decisions are reached through best practice, rather than from collective pressure.

These tools are also important to limit groupthink in a societal context. As we write this book, the limits of free speech are being tested daily around the world, and psychological safety is, in some contexts, becoming more and more difficult to find. By actively bringing these tools into practice in whatever contexts we can, we show how calling out the need for psychological safety, being more open to dissent, reviewing decisions, and allowing for devil's advocates makes us all more intentional and improves our interactions, whatever context they're in.

PART IV

Integrity

CHAPTER 15

Living Our Values

"To thine own self be true, and it must follow, as the night the day, thou canst not then be false to any man."
—William Shakespeare, *Hamlet*

Fred Rogers—or as most of us know him, Mister Rogers—is the most famous American children's TV host. Between 1968 and 2001, he taped more than 1,000 episodes of *Mister Rogers' Neighborhood*, changed the lives of generations of kids, received more than 40 honorary degrees, and most recently, was memorialized by Tom Hanks on the big screen.[1]

While many of us know him as a relentlessly kind, ethical, and immutable giant, this is an image he became, not one he was born with. In the 1950s, Rogers was studying to be a Presbyterian minister. He saw a children's TV program that featured adults throwing pies at each others' faces, trying to get a laugh out of their young audience. He couldn't quite put his finger on why, but it made him upset. There was something about the program that missed the point. As he later said: "I saw this new thing called television, and I saw people throwing pies in each other's faces, and I thought, 'This could be a wonderful tool for education! Why is it being used this way?' So I said to my parents, 'You know, I don't think I'll go into seminary right away. I think I'll go into television.'"[2]

Fred Rogers knew that the program he saw was misaligned with his view of the world, what he cared about, and what he thought it could be. And he believed that TV could be a powerful force in improving children's lives. Over the next decade, he learned to clarify his values of respect, tolerance, and excellence, and he was on his way to creating something that changed the world. His integrity gave rise to his intention and supported the achievement of his goals. He may not have become extremely wealthy from his work, but he touched the lives of millions and continues to have a profound effect on the world.

Integrity: The Seeds of Intention

Often when we talk about intention, we center on goals like healthier eating and career achievement. These are important to us—and statistically, they're probably important to you, too—but they may not be primary values. Your strongest values may lie in nurturing your friendships, maximizing your travel opportunities, or even in wanting to break a world record in holding your breath underwater—you do you! Though much of our society seems aligned around what we should choose to strive for, no one can identify your own values for you. In this chapter, we look at some ideas on how to identify what matters *most* to you, but first we explore how our values relate to integrity.

Integrity is acting in a way that's aligned with what you believe. Walking the talk, doing what you say and saying what you do, standing up for what you think is right—these are all common expressions of integrity.

Integrity has made its way into the five ingredients of intention because we simply cannot act with intention if our values are a mystery to us. To be intentional, we must first know what we want and why we want it. Only then, once we understand our values, can we work to manifest them on a daily basis. This directly connects to how engaged we are in the world, which brings us back again to our topic of increasing disengagement. What if this upward trend of disengagement has something to do with our confusion about our values—or how we act on them?

How Do We Identify Our Values?

In his widely read *New York Times* article, "The Moral Bucket List," cultural commentator David Brooks muses on the individuals who can't help but radiate "an inner light."[3] These people aren't necessarily successful; they can come from a myriad of backgrounds, lifestyles, and occupations. They exude what Brooks refers to as "eulogy virtues." When we die, our loved ones won't eulogize our work accomplishments or high grades. They'll speak of our core qualities: our patience, courage, or generosity. These persona-defining qualities are our eulogy virtues. The difficulty in identifying our eulogy virtues is that we're often pushed toward résumé virtues. Résumé virtues, as Brooks explains, are "the skills you bring to the marketplace." We receive ample praise for traits like efficiency—but delivering work on time is only a surface-level aspect of our personhood. While it can feel good to build these traits into our idea of selfhood, we must remember to take the time to nurture the traits that will define us long after we're gone. This may mean to first of all identify them.

> As a personal exercise, let's imagine that it's your 100th birthday and your life and achievements are going to be celebrated by family, friends, and colleagues. Take a moment to think about what you would like these people to say about you at the party, how you would like to be celebrated and appreciated (maybe even gently roasted). Actually close your eyes and picture the scene. Maybe it's an outdoor picnic on a nice warm day with a light breeze blowing. All of the people that you love and respect are gathered to hear about you and your life and one by one, your best friends and closest family members get up to give a toast to you. What would you want them to say? Would you want them to talk about your curiosity and eagerness to learn? Your faith and loyalty? What about how you helped many or served as an inspiration to others?

This seemingly simple exercise is actually quite profound. Spending a few minutes thinking about this will help you to identify what you believe is important about yourself and what you appreciate most about who you are. You might be surprised at what you realize here, and what it tells you about how you are living your life.

Other exercises in the following chapters can help you to further identify your core values, the traits that should guide both your daily actions and grand life decisions. Identifying these values is the first step to creating integrity, and in so doing, supporting your ability to act intentionally.

Growing into Integrity

As you explore your values in the next few chapters, strive to remember that values, just like us, change with time. Our understanding of right and wrong evolves as we experience the world and gain new perspectives. This change doesn't mean we were once moral failures—change is often proof that we're giving it our best shot and just like our small-*b* and big-*B* beliefs, the evolution of our values speaks to our ability to learn and adapt.

> 90% of people agree that their core values have evolved over time.

We aren't born with integrity. We must actively grow it within ourselves. No one exemplifies this practice better, or on a grander scale, than the ancient king Ashoka.

Ashoka, an Indian Emperor in the 3rd century BCE, experienced one of the most radical shifts in philosophy ever documented in a political leader. Ashoka was the grandson of Chandragupta Maurya, the founder of the Mauryan Dynasty, and despite having several brothers, Ashoka was crowned king in 269 BCE. He was rumored to have orchestrated the killings of his siblings, including the rightful heir, in order to seize the throne. After his ascension, Ashoka began forcefully expanding his grandfather's empire. He conquered much of Southeast Asia, ruthless in his quest. But everything changed the day he conquered Kalinga.

Kalinga was on the eastern side of the subcontinent and it was a province ruled not by monarchy, but by a form of parliamentary democracy—an unusual level of freedom at the time. The population was largely Buddhist, and Ashoka's practiced army conquered it easily, in the process killing more than 100,000 Kalingan soldiers and deporting many more.

But on entering his new land, Ashoka was moved by the extent of destruction his army had caused. One legend tells of Ashoka walking around his newly conquered province, stopped by the sound of soft chanting. It was the monk Upagupta, reciting "Buddham saranam gacchami," a mantra translated as "I take refuge in Lord Buddha." Akosha asked the man what he was chanting. He wanted to learn more about Buddhism, the practice this man turned to in the face of total destruction.

Soon after, in a now-famous speech, Ashoka explained the shift in his perspective the conquest of Kalinga had caused. "What have I done? If this is a victory, what's a defeat then? Is this a victory or a defeat? Is this justice or injustice? Is it gallantry or a rout? Is it valor to kill innocent children and women? Did I do it to widen the empire and for prosperity or to destroy the other's kingdom and splendor?"[4]

In response to his decimation of Kalinga, Ashoka became a devout Buddhist and began acting with greater integrity and intention. In an attempt to make up for his violent past, he dramatically changed his reign to favor peace and prosperity. He gave up on expanding his empire. He started to provide better services for his people, like hospitals and schools. He traveled around the subcontinent erecting statues of Buddha, as a testament to nonviolence. He even changed the nature of kingdom in Southeast Asia—no longer were kings appointed by divine right, free to rule how they wished. It became common practice for Southeast Asian kings to rule in association with the Buddhist community.

Ashoka's Lasting Legacy

While the Mauryan Empire lasted only 50 years after his death, Ashoka's legacy is far more powerful than an extension of his dynasty. He's remembered as one of the most influential leaders of all time, and his impact remains strong to this day. After his Buddhist conversion, Ashoka created the Ashoka Chakra—a wheel of righteousness. The Ashoka Chakra was accepted as the national symbol of India. You've likely seen it before: ever since the country's independence in 1947, it has featured in the center of the Indian flag.

The wheel itself symbolizes integrity. Each of the 24 spokes represents a different virtue that speaks to rights and responsibilities that exist regardless of religion, language, or caste. The spokes include peace, forgiveness, fraternity, sacrifice, and justice—the kinds of values that we won't receive awards for, but will be eulogized at our funerals. They all flow from a common center that, while everything around it turns, holds still.

Although change is inevitable, having a strong center helps us to ensure that the direction we go in aligns with who we are. Think about which values make up the spokes of your wheel—remembering that they can shift and change, while your center holds true.

Know also that by living your values fully, you can inspire others to do the same. Chances are we won't all get the opportunity to establish peace in warring regions and help spread a global religion, but we can all affect change in the parts of the world we inhabit. By radiating our intentional values, we help others to discover theirs and to build their own sense of integrity.

CHAPTER 16

How to Uncover Your Values

"Your vision will become clear only when you can look into your own heart. Who looks outside, dreams; who looks inside, awakes."

—Carl Jung

Meet Anika—a young software developer working at a trendy tech startup. This is her first job out of college, and she's there to kill it. She goes in every day, makes a cup of steaming coffee, and sits at her desk. The hustle and bustle of the office fades into the background, and she becomes completely immersed in her code. Her entire world becomes a matrix of functions and algorithms.

The company that Anika works for is one of the hottest startups in the country. Everyone says it's likely to be the next billion-dollar unicorn. All you have to do is spend a few minutes at the office to feel the optimism like static in the air. They're out to do something really hard, and they just might have a shot.

When Anika first joined as a fresh graduate a few years ago, she was bubbling with enthusiasm. She couldn't believe how far she had come. It was all like a dream. But as the months and years passed, something began to gnaw at her. The product she was working on had taken a slow turn from the grandiose vision she had joined the startup to support and was becoming something else. It was starting to feel like a cash grab for investors. She can temporarily push away the gnawing, but it can't be ignored. She knows it's there. The passion for coding and for the meaning of the project that had driven her when she first started has begun to dim like a lighthouse being engulfed by fog. Anika sees it happening, but she sustains her effort with a burning ambition.

Maybe it's normal, she tells herself. Maybe that's just how the real world works. And after all, just a few more years and she'll be a senior engineer. It's true that this job has chipped away at her social life and made it impossible to date or have any hobbies. But that's just what it takes to succeed, right? Isn't that what it takes to be a high performer? We all act sometimes as if this version of reality is true, even if both our intuition and the research say no.

We started this book by talking about disengagement—would you call Anika disengaged? It certainly doesn't look like she is—she's as productive as ever and even experienced managers would hesitate to make this call. That's because disengagement is a feeling, not necessarily a behavior. Anika might look like the best performer in the world from the outside, but only she knows how well she's actually performing relative to her own standards. She's the only one who knows what high performance looks like for her. The salient point here is that whether we take the time to understand our own values or not, they'll seep into our experience of the world and the decisions we make.

Let's say that more plainly. No matter how much outward success we might achieve, we're all prone to disengagement creep. And one of the big cracks disengagement can creep in through is our value system. Living and organizing our life according to priorities that are not our own is an affront to our sense of integrity—and difficult to make peace with in the long term. We can "be pragmatic" and do what needs to be done for a time, but this will ultimately come back to haunt us for one very simple reason: we're not achieving our own goals. We've replaced them with convenient goals, perhaps even socially desirable ones. But if they're not our own, and we're alienating ourselves from our own life, we're no longer being a Main Character.

Feelings of disengagement are a signal that we may need some *value clarification*. Value clarification is the process of understanding the set of priorities that drives you. Not just the ones you would like to be your priorities, but the ones that are reflected in how you spend your time, and more importantly, how you react emotionally to the ways you spend your time. Value clarification allows us to get to know ourselves better, so we can best steer our daily choices as well as the course of our lives. From organizational change management[1] to healthcare,[2] value clarification or alignment has been shown to drastically improve decision-making processes as well as the outcomes of the decisions taken. Yet, despite how important it is, value clarification is something most of us assume we don't really need. To understand the intuition behind why this might happen, and how we could overcome it, we can turn to the world of artificial intelligence (AI)—one place where value clarification is a very obvious and immediate problem, and perhaps even an existential threat.

The Complexity of Values through AI

There's a strange kind of infinity to AI. While humans (and other animals) have evolved to use tools to accomplish tasks, we've never really had tools that decide which tasks should be accomplished—in a very real sense replacing human agency. Its increasing level of independence from us makes AI inherently very different from a hammer or a saw that must be wielded by a human for it to work. AI makes its own decisions, outside of our view, and more alarmingly, even outside of our comprehension.

This increasing independence means that AI needs less and less input from us. But as the amount of input changes, the quality of that input has to increase if we want AI to actually be a useful tool. This is where AI value alignment comes in, aligning intention with ensuing action. While swinging a hammer invariably produces a large force in the direction of the swing, AI's complexity means that the intention–action gap can be far, far wider. Therefore, defining the priorities within which the AI must act is critical. And when we define priorities, we also define a set of values.

AI value alignment refers to building artificial intelligence that can act in accordance with the goals and interests of those who created it—and doing this is really, really, *really* hard. For one, imagine having to distill the entirety of human values into a single set of these that you give to an AI. It's a bit like reducing the *Mona Lisa* to a 10-by-10 pixel image. The gist might be there, but the defining qualitative details are gone. Then, of course, there's the issue of conflicting value systems. How do you encode those? Finally, even if you do somehow manage to translate all of that self-contradictory complexity into a single list, how do you translate that list into a series of concrete rules and priorities? In other words, a huge part of the difficulty in AI alignment has to do with value clarification.

To more thoroughly illustrate just how difficult this is, let's look at a classic thought experiment of AI alignment gone wrong from Nick Bostom's "Ethical Issues in Advanced Artificial Intelligence."[3] Bostom asks us to imagine a powerful AI programmed with the task of creating paper clips. This machine has one single value: make paper clips. Everything else is a tool used to achieve this single value.

The machine may start by suggesting simple ways to optimize the existing production of paper clips. As it learns a bit more, it might suggest an entirely new process that's 10 times faster. Then, as it starts to become more proficient than a human, it might start to implement new strategies without even asking. In fact, if the machine isn't programmed to preserve human life, and assuming it has enough power over its environment, it will eventually start to use any and all surroundings to manufacture paper clips. The only logical conclusion is that the AI will eventually transform as much of the universe as it can into paper clips. This isn't an AI gone rogue or malfunctioning. It's an AI doing exactly what it was told. While it's called "alignment," the issue here isn't that the AI is misaligned with the set of values it was given. Rather, it wasn't given a nuanced set of values that reflects its creators' values (like the one about not turning puppies into paper clips).

Another—much more realistic—example is the increasingly popular idea of self-driving cars. If you're writing the software for one of these cars, you have the unpleasant but critical task of deciding on the procedure for crashes. Of course, you start with the obvious values: it's bad when people die in car crashes. But how should the car best follow the goal of minimal human deaths? Should the car be programmed to swerve to the side to avoid hitting a pedestrian, even if it endangers the life of the driver by hitting a nearby tree? What if there are others on board, or the pedestrian crossing the road is a group of children? Reducing our values to a set of instructions is often insufficient to capture the complexity of the real world.

These aren't technology issues. They're issues with technology, but they are largely nontechnical in nature. They're about value clarification. The problem of AI value alignment is, to a large extent, the problem of human value clarification. How can we teach something to do what we are not even fully conscious of? It may seem obvious or trivial to tell AI "Don't kill living beings to make paper clips" or even "Don't ever kill" (in line with Isaac Asimov's famous First Law of Robotics). But these instructions fail to capture the full nuance of our human values. They're no match for complex situations like self-driving cars picking which set of pedestrians to crash into.

All of this is critically important to our discussion about integrity because AI value alignment can tell us several things about human integrity:

- ◆ If you want to act with integrity, instead of pursuing random optimization goals like making paper clips or getting promoted, you need to clarify a set of values.
- ◆ Value clarification is hard. Each of our value systems is immensely complex, contradictory, culturally dependent, and situation-specific. You're the only one who can decipher it for yourself.
- ◆ While some of our values are explicit and easy to encode, other values are hard for us to see in ourselves, and may even surprise us.

How to Clarify Your Own Values

Most of us claim to know our value system, but it's likely a little murkier than we'd like to believe. If our values guide our everyday actions, as they should, which values are we putting the major part of our time toward? Whether our chosen values are religious or secular, most of us agree more or less on a few basics. We abide by the classics: do not murder, do not steal, do not defraud. But our values go much deeper than not killing others.

Now, there's no need to jump straight into deciding which values will govern our decisions until our final days, creating an indeterminate legacy that will live on long after we do. Let's start off easy, with the basics: what *are* values?

Professors and social psychologists Shalom Schwartz and Wolfgang Bilsky conducted a literature review in 1987 to find out just that. Based on a breadth of previous research, they concluded that values are "(a) concepts or beliefs, (b) about desirable end states or behaviors, (c) that transcend specific situations, (d) guide selection or evaluation of behavior and events, and (e) are ordered by relative importance."[4] In summary, our values are beliefs that we hold beyond specific contexts and that determine the choices we make.

Now that we understand the nature of values, we can move onto value clarification—figuring out our own values. We can see value clarification as an ongoing process of development of defining what we value (what is important for us) and how we act on these values in our day-to-day life.[5] Why do you spend heaps of overtime at the office when you value your family life? Why do you skip your lunchtime walk if health is one of your top priorities? Value clarification can highlight the "why" behind our decisions, from moving to a new city to what to pick for breakfast, and this clarity allows us to be more intentional and act with integrity.

An easy starting point for determining your values is beginning with a value classification tool like the one we discuss for teams in Chapter 18. If it's been a year or more since you last clarified your values—putting language to your deeply held beliefs—revisit them. Just like us, our values are ever-evolving. But another way to clarify your values that is purely personal is borrowing an interrogative technique from Toyota Motors: the five whys.

The father of the famous Toyota Production System, Taiichi Ohno, developed the five whys approach to better practice understanding the root causes of production mishaps. It wasn't enough to say an engine piece was malfunctioning because the machine built it improperly. He encouraged his employees to explore these inevitable problems by asking "why?" five consecutive times, each time digging into the cause of the reason given in answer to the previous why.[6] Five was often enough to get to the root, though it could always be extended as needed.

Changing its application from the shop floor to our own behaviors, start by taking an action you do every day. As you ask "why" five times, make sure you dig deep. Each "why" should require a good deal of thought. Try not to jump to easy conclusions; eliminate any preconceived notions you might have about why you do what you do in order to really get at the deeply held value. The five whys technique allows us to reverse engineer our values.

> Try it for yourself by taking something that you do or believe in (it can be as simple as brushing your teeth or the type of shampoo you prefer to use, or as complicated as why you don't eat meat or why you read the books you read) and ask yourself why you do or believe in that thing. Write down your first-level answer and then ladder down by asking yourself why that is the case. Do it five times and you might be surprised at what you discover about yourself.

For example, why don't you steal? You might answer that it's because stealing causes harm to others. But why is that bad? Because you're infringing on their personal property? Why is that bad? Because everyone has the right to personal property? Why?

Interestingly, when we do this exercise, we might find that certain things we consider to be personal values actually fall in one of the following categories of value origins:

- ◆ *Social norms*: Rules created and enforced by the society we live in. Many of our values might be rooted in compliance to these social norms—perhaps you don't truly value a clothed society, but you don't want to be rejected by society for embracing nudism.[7]
- ◆ *Emotional states*: The result of transitory feelings that influence our sense of priority. Perhaps you believe in environmental conservation, but you're willing to take long flights when wanderlust strikes.[8]
- ◆ *Authority figures*: We tend to put trust in authority figures, like parents, teachers, coaches, bosses, public figures, or religious leaders. Perhaps you believe strongly in the concept of regular charitable donations because your parents and rabbi have instilled it in you.[9]

If your values can be traced to these categories, or other external factors, that's not to say they're inferior or bad. But understanding the provenance of our values is necessary. It's only by better understanding our values that we can intentionally align our actions with them.

Value identification is so important that we'd like to suggest another exercise here. This is called the "Best Possible Self" exercise and has been used as a psychological intervention in a variety of contexts.[10] Here, we'll use it to clarify our values.

1. **Visualize:** Sit down in a calm (and safe) place, close your eyes and picture a future for yourself that has gone as well as it possibly could. You've worked hard and achieved all of your life goals. Make sure what you're imagining is achievable with hard work and dedication.

2. **Detail:** Take a piece of paper and write down details about what you've achieved in various domains— family, relationships, hobbies, career, fitness, and so on. Be as specific as you can be.

3. **Identify:** Once you're done, think about the values that this future you has. What matters most to future you? What does future you stand for? How does future you prioritize your day?

4. **Compare:** Now compare the values of your future self to your current values. Are there any big differences that strike you?

5. **Take Action:** What changes do you think you might need to make to create more alignment between these two versions of you?

One weird assumption about values is that our current values are, almost by definition, the ones we want to have. But, as the previous exercise shows and as we see in the coming chapters, this assumption doesn't always hold.

Our overarching goal here is to better understand our own value systems. Doing this is the first step in developing integrity. Integrity is ultimately about aligning our actions with our values, but that's hard to do if we're not sure what our values are. Being sure of our values can re-engage us with our lives and allow us to create a sense of well-being and satisfaction that comes from authentic choices. It allows us to have more authentic relationships with others. Even when our values don't align, this centeredness allows us to find ways to talk about value differences with others from a kind and confident place (the center of the Ashoka Chakra we spoke of in Chapter 15). Finally, equipped with a better understanding of our values, we can take better action and chart our trek through complex waters with the most updated map.

CHAPTER 17

When Values Conflict

"Do I contradict myself? Very well, then I contradict myself, I am large, I contain multitudes."

—Walt Whitman

We hope you've now identified some of the values that drive you and perhaps some actions that are better aligned with those values. But you probably realize that some of your identified values actually conflict with each other. You value achievement and so work very hard at your job, but you also value your family. You're often torn between spending time with them and being present at work. What do you do?

The Benefits of Value Tension

Weirdly enough, the tension that you feel between opposing values can be a good thing, and here are three reasons why:

First, tension between our values helps us to build our agency and identity in our formative years. Psychologist Seth Schwartz and his team at the University of Miami have argued that an essential part of the process of becoming an adult, which stretches deep into the 20s (or beyond), is finding resolutions to internal value conflicts. This helps us do something called *individualization*—the process of creating our own identities.[1]

131

Second, value conflict stretches our cognitive limits. Research from Princeton University on the neural correlates (associated brain patterns or activity) of moral conflict shows that solving these conflicts is hard.[2] It requires brain circuitry that supports more cognitive and more emotional processes—at the intersection of value conflict. Our internal value conflicts may even represent a tug of war between diverse brain circuitries. Wrestling with our values actively engages these different parts of our brain, strengthening our ability to make complex decisions.

Third, as argued by New York University professor and *Coddling of the American Mind* author Jonathan Haidt in a paper on values,[3] having a larger pool of internal value conflicts may allow us to understand a larger number of people. In his work, Haidt has proposed that there are five core psychological systems we might use to form value judgments: one that looks for harm and care, one that looks for fairness and reciprocity, one for ingroup and loyalty, one for authority and respect, and one for purity and sanctity. People rely differently on these systems. Someone with less moral conflict might lean strongly into one or two of these systems, and be unable to understand a person with a more nuanced and broad evaluation of the world. By having more perspectives, we can more easily understand views that are different from our own.

So while internal value conflict can feel uncomfortable or confusing, it can serve a useful purpose. Without it, we wouldn't know who we are or how to relate to others.

Reconciling Intentions

But what do you do if you have two intentions that are in direct conflict with one another? It's all well and good to say that this might be useful from a developmental point of view, but it can still feel uncomfortable! One way to solve this is to dig down to understand your root intentions. Once we understand these primary drivers, we can implement a secondary set of related intentions from there. That way, even if the secondary intentions don't align with each other, they will still align with the primary intention. For example, maybe you value living a healthy lifestyle because you want to increase your lifespan. But perhaps you occasionally slip up on your healthy lifestyle by missing sleep or going for drinks. These activities can still serve your primary goal of living a long life—a strong social network has been shown to improve our longevity.[4] Even though social activities with a couple of drinks might require going against our healthy lifestyle of no alcohol consumption, these two goals both serve the same root purpose: living longer.

To intentionally make these value trade-offs, we need to understand our core values. As long as our other intentions are aligned with a root goal, it doesn't matter if they occasionally conflict. Going out with friends for beers and wings (or your version of going against one of your values) every once in a while won't blow up your healthy lifestyle plans. Ultimately, your goal should be to aim for alignment, not rigid conformity. But sometimes alignment isn't possible, and you have to make a choice.

One particularly high-profile example of this is Naomi Osaka's decision to withdraw from the French Open in 2021. Osaka was the second-highest ranked female tennis player at the time, the highest-paid female athlete in the world, and she was leading the competition. In her press statement, Osaka explained she had begun to struggle with depression after her win at the 2018 U.S. Open and was stepping back due to mental health concerns.

Dozens of news outlets dedicated headlines to reporting on Osaka's withdrawal, and op-eds were divided on whether she was to be scorned or supported for her decision. In the days leading up to her withdrawal, Osaka faced criticism for her decision to skip post-match media sessions, leading to the threat of being expelled from all four Grand Slam tournaments and a $15,000 charge from the tournament referee if she refused to participate. She was faced with the choice of paying the hefty fine, withdrawing from the tournament, or participating in media sessions to the detriment of her mental health. Onlookers were stunned by her choice to withdraw.

For many, Osaka's decision seemed to go against her ambitions for inexplicable reasons. Pulling out of a Grand Slam tournament for mental health reasons led reporters and writers to call her "petulant," "narcissistic," and a "diva."[5] But those who supported Osaka's position understood the importance of putting the value of her health first. Only by taking necessary care of herself could she come back stronger.

Osaka's decision illustrates a difficult lesson in achieving our goals—we're not always going to move directly toward them. In a way, this is like sailing—it would be easy if all we had to do is to raise our sails, allow the wind to fill them, and float off to our destination.[6] Unfortunately, the wind doesn't always blow in the direction we're going. What do sailors do then? They "tack" into the wind. Angling the bow of their boat into the direction of the wind allows the boat to take a zigzag approach, sailing into the wind through a series of sharp turns.

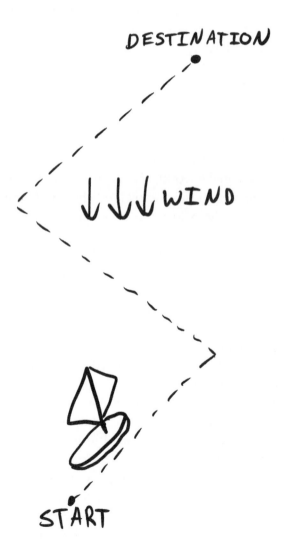

When we're moving in the direction of our intentions, running directly at them is not always best. There are many scenarios in which it's better to work toward our goals in steps, some of which might not be in the exact direction we want to go. If your goal is to run a marathon, daily runs take you straight toward your goal. But you can't leave it at that—you also want to focus on nutrition and flexibility and strength training. If you get injured, the best step toward your goal is resting, ensuring you heal as much as possible before getting back on the treadmill. And sometimes, just like Osaka, you have to take a step back before you can move forward. As Osaka posted on social media, announcing her planned return to tennis in 2024, "I don't think there's a perfectly correct path to take in life, but I always felt that if you move forward with good intentions you'll find your way eventually."[7]

The Power of Diverse Dissent

Making decisions that prioritize our values (or that align with our integrity) is difficult enough by ourselves, but it is even harder when those around us hold differing values. In a group context, people are often faced with the conundrum of having to choose between fitting into the group (social cohesion) and their own values. So what should we do in these situations?

A significant amount of research supports that having diverse values on a team is a net positive, as long as those values are allowed to flourish in a useful way. A 2018 study from management professor Amy Randel[8] and her colleagues found that teams with "inclusive leadership" allowed team members to express their individuality in a way that increased creativity and productivity.

What does an inclusive leader look like? According to their research, there are five positive behaviors that inclusive leaders engage in:

- Making members of the team feel supported.
- Making members of the team feel there is justice and equity in the team.
- Giving members a chance to engage in shared decision-making.
- Encouraging members to contribute in a unique/diverse way.
- Helping members contribute their unique skills and points of view.

Just like in our personal values, contrasting values in a group context can be both challenging and beneficial. A natural outcome of allowing teams to express the unique values of each team member means being open to points of view that are sometimes drastically different. In fact, situations of dissent can actually push organizations to be more effective. Research has shown that teams that contain dissenters make better decisions.

Take a study from The University of Göttingen, which tested 135 three-person groups on their collective decision-making.[9] Each group was asked to make a decision using separate pieces of information that were distributed among the different team members. Groups with no dissent hardly ever got to the right solution, but the groups that included dissenters were more successful in reaching the correct answer. The researchers even found that this effect was modulated by the discussion intensity (assessed by three indicators: average proportion of information shared, average repetition rate of information, and discussion time), showing, in effect, that the more noise the dissenter made, the more likely the group was to reach the right decision. Without dissent, we're not exposing teams to the challenges that will help them become better teams.

While it can be easy to fall prey to groupthink and do what's expected of us, each of our perspectives is valuable to a wider group. When we are working in groups, we need to encourage the members of our teams to be individuals, especially in circumstances where not allowing this can cause harm, both to the person and to the long-term interests of the group. At the same time, allowing too much dissent can stifle progress, so what are we to do?

Set the North Star

As we saw earlier, our context can have a significant impact on our values. As members of teams, we impact that context daily. Being intentional about that impact is an important component to helping create an organization where dissent is valued. The environment will shape the values of the people in it and you have a role to play in building that environment.

As leaders, we are also called on to help set the ultimate destination for our collective voyage. Yes, we can and should tack into the wind, but to do so we need to know where we're going. This is not just a question of good strategic planning, but a need to have a vision for the future and a clear sense of what the overarching goals might be.

As a quick visual exercise here, try thinking of a situation where there are conflicting values either inside you or between different team members. Divide a piece of paper in two halves and write those different perspectives on each half of the paper. Now draw two overlapping circles, with one value or position in each, but a large middle ground between them. What lies in that middle ground? That is the place where agreement is found. Perhaps one person wants the team to focus on recruiting new employees and the other wants the team to concentrate on retention of current colleagues. The obvious overlap is in the desire to have the best people in the best roles possible. This won't necessarily solve the difference of perspective, but it will show that we're all headed to the same destination (or highlight that we're not in some cases, which is a useful learning in and of itself).

Pick Alignment over Consensus

In groups, we often try to achieve consensus, even if that's not necessarily the best goal. As with our individual intentions, alignment (even begrudging agreement) can be better than consensus. Oftentimes, achieving consensus requires watering down an idea so much that it loses all creativity and innovation. In our experience working with high-performing teams in various industries, we've found that groups striving for consensus often get bogged down in interminable meetings. In the end, they finally agree on a bland objective, or reach a solution that isn't that interesting, bold, or challenging to the status quo. But teams with a strong leader who aims for alignment rather than consensus are able to be more decisive. Not only that, but by showing integrity, teams that tack toward value alignment tend to become stronger, more resilient teams.

Leading with Integrity

Integrity in leaders affects the entire team. Research has shown that effective leaders are ones who show a high degree of alignment between their words and their actions. We want to feel that those leading us are intrinsically motivated to do the things they're asking us to help with, and also that they are acting in ways that are seen as ethical.

We are not presuming that "integrity" and "ethical behavior" are the same thing (some people out there might have the priority of being a jerk), but for the most part, the field of behavioral ethics has shown us that they do coincide. People want to see themselves as ethical. They generally want to be a good person. They can, of course, stray away from ethical behavior in the interest of some gain, but they tend to think of that as a sacrifice of sorts and feel bad about it. As it turns out, however, acting outside of your zone of integrity hurts those around you as well.

The trickle-down effects of ethical leadership can be felt at every level of organizational structure. Top executives can influence managers, and managers can influence their subordinates. But research shows that the greatest impact comes from direct supervisors; employees see their supervisors as embodiments of workplace values, more so than high-level executives. When an employee's direct supervisor acts with integrity, so do they. This mimicry can be largely explained by social learning theory and social exchange theory: we learn social behaviors by imitating others, and we act in accordance with how others treat us—when our bosses demonstrate integrity, we imitate and reciprocate.

Not only does ethical leadership make everyone around us more ethical, ethical leadership can also improve engagement. A team of researchers from Yonsei University investigated the impact of ethical leadership on fatigue at work, exploring the dynamic across 259 employees in South Korea.[10] Their investigation focused specifically on emotional exhaustion at work—that chronic feeling of depletion when you're in a demanding work environment.

The researchers found that leaders who demonstrated ethical leadership could lower the levels of emotional exhaustion in their employees. This was because, around the leaders with ethical leadership style, employees used less emotional effort when interacting with their peers and superiors. And, as expected, less effort spent on social interactions turned into higher levels of engagement and productivity for the employees.

There are pretty obvious connections here between these points and the broader societal challenge of disengagement that we've discussed since the opening pages of the book. More ethical leadership, more opportunities to dissent and express differing values, a shared goal of alignment without necessarily forcing consensus—all of these would have a positive effect on the world. As with the other ingredients to intention in this book, by working on these things for ourselves and through the groups we participate in, we're bettering us all. In the next chapter, we look into how you can best get to know the values of others, and in doing so, build toward the magic of shared intentions.

CHAPTER 18

Know Thy Team

"Could a greater miracle take place than for us to look through each other's eyes for an instant?"
—Henry David Thoreau

Prior to becoming a chief human resources officer, Mike often ran workshops for executives. One of these workshops was on empathy, and it included an exercise that always bewildered the participants.

In this exercise, the executives wrote down their top three values, chosen from a set list of potential values like honesty, courage, vision, humility, and efficiency. Then they would be asked to think about a colleague in the workshop that they knew well and do the same exercise for that person, identifying that colleague's top three values. Time and time again there were two key takeaways: First, most of the executives struggled to come up with their top three values and found it much easier to identify a colleague's top values. Second, most participants were wildly incorrect about their colleague's top values. Only rarely would someone identify even one value that a colleague had chosen for themselves in their top three.

In the discussions that followed, teams often came away stronger and more empathic toward one another, even when their core values weren't aligned. The act of talking through each other's values brought them together and often had positive knock-on effects in terms of their culture and alignment. This aligns with research on teams that finds that a key process in team formation is building team members' awareness of their own and each other's values. In a study carried out by educational psychologist Bruce Tuckman, he showed that sharing information is a key ingredient to team formation—the first stage of team building. Tuckman noted that an individual team member's behavior at this stage is driven by a desire to be accepted by the other team members.[1] Feeling understood and known is a necessary precondition for healthy relationships, whether it's in the workplace, or even a family.

How Well Do We Really Know Others?

Like Mike's workshop showed its participants, we don't know one another nearly as well as we might think. In fact, we tend to think it's easier to know others than for others to know us. So a further benefit of this exercise is highlighting our own hubris—are others really as knowable as we believe they are? In a classic 2001 study, psychologist Emily Pronin introduced the "illusion of asymmetric insight."[2]

In a series of experiments, Pronin and a team of researchers from Stanford University investigated how we perceive the difference between knowing others and being known. Of course we are not talking about being fully known—this is something that may not be possible even for ourselves. We mean a form of knowing that demonstrates accurate understanding of others' qualities, style, and preferences.

Why do we tend to think we know others better than they know us? It's partially because we read a lot into what we do know of other people—we extrapolate from the small amount of information that we have—and think that we've got it right. Researchers in one of Pronin's studies, for example, found that participants thought observable traits were more telling of their friends than internal traits. This means that an individual would think that the messiness level of their roommate (an observable trait) said a lot about their roommate's true nature. But the same individual would ascertain that their own messiness level didn't reveal all that much about their true self. This is the cognitive bias known as asymmetric insight in action.

Think back to Mike's empathy workshop—the executives thought they knew their colleagues quite well, but as it almost always turned out, they were reading into observable characteristics and forgetting to account for the unobservable qualities of their peers. In fact, the Stanford researchers found that when asked to write down descriptions of themselves and their close friends, participants would write far more internal characteristics for themselves, and far more observable characteristics for their friends—but both were presented as the "true self." The authors of the study remarked that their participants "appeared to function as naive Freudians, willing to infer the deeper significance of each other's incidental gestures, tone of voice, or offhand remarks."[3] It can be easy to forget there's more to our friends and colleagues than meets the eye, but that undersight comes with a high cost when it comes to living and working together authentically.

Not only do we highlight external characteristics for others and internal ones for ourselves, but we often see other people through our own understanding of the world. This results in stereotyping and mental projection when assessing other people's motivations and values.[4] Another way to say this is that we put other people in our shoes instead of putting ourselves in theirs. This is backed up by a wealth of research that has shown that when we infer others' values, we often just replicate our own.[5] In short, we often forget to account for how different people are from ourselves.

The Mistake of Assuming Values

So we're not great at understanding the values of others, but why is that a problem? Let's look a little closer to find out how things can go awry, starting with those people we believe are like us. If we judge someone to be similar to us—even in a small way, like sharing the same sense of humor—we tend to project our own attitudes and desires onto them. In other words, we automatically assume that we have far more than just a sense of humor in common. But when we interact with those who are dissimilar, who do not appear to share much with us, we tend to project stereotypes onto them. These stereotypes, pulled from our stock internal ideas about others (think about what you believe about librarians and football players, for example, although there are much worse stereotypes out there), are used to infer the internal workings of people who are different from us.[6] Our brains love to take these simple shortcuts: essentially believing that everyone like us thinks like us, and everyone not like us thinks the way we think they do.

When we're trying to understand the inner workings of our colleagues, we can be quick to use these shortcuts. We assume that our co-worker—who looks like us, dresses like us, and makes the same jokes as us—has the same values we do. In reality, these similarities don't indicate anything deeper than the fact that we are in the same income bracket and shop at the same store. On the other hand, we might look at colleagues who differ from us and assume we know their values without further thought. We might assume a co-worker who is much older or younger than us subscribes to the stereotypes of their generation—perhaps we believe they're bigoted or lazy—instead of having their own values shaped by extrinsic and intrinsic factors we are not aware of.

To make matters worse, not only do we assume the values of others, but we tend to undervalue others and overvalue ourselves. The explanation for this is that it's easy for our minds to assume the best of ourselves and the worst of those around us. In a 2017 study, Ben Tappin and Ryan McKay at the University of London asked 270 participants to rate themselves and others on core traits like morality, agency, and sociability.[7] When it came to morality, virtually everyone inflated their moral qualities. Everyone considered themselves to be moral actors, but estimated that the average person wasn't all that moral.[8] Tappin and McKay found that this wasn't even due to self-esteem—it's not that we think we're better than others. We just believe we're morally superior.

Assuming the worst of others' intentions is referred to as the *extrinsic incentive bias*. We think we're motivated by intrinsic factors, like the intellectual appeal of a job, while others are motivated by extrinsic factors, like higher wages. No one is quite sure why we tend to do this—perhaps external incentives are more concrete, or maybe we want to see ourselves as better than our average peers.[9] Whatever the reasons, knowing that our brains are playing these tricks on us can help us overcome them. If we're more intentional in how we think about others, we can override these unhelpful assumptions— much like we know that when we're carrying a box into the basement that we need to slow down and make sure we step firmly on each step so that we don't end up on the injured list.

How to Know Thy Team

Teams don't need to share all of the same values—and as we've discussed, it's actually better if they don't. But to function at their best, team members should be aware of each other's values. Clarifying values isn't just about discovery, but about adjusting preconceived notions.

How do we put greater value transparency into practice in our teams? Here are three steps to facilitate team openness:

STEP 1: HELP TEAM MEMBERS DISCOVER THEIR OWN VALUES

The first step in creating an open, informed culture is helping team members get to know themselves. The workshops Mike ran used a fairly simple set of tools to help participants discover their own values. They would start with 60 cards, each with a one-word value on it (like honesty, courage, excellence, and achievement). Participants were asked to divide the cards into three sets, ranking them as important, very important, or most important. Then they would take the most important pile and choose their top three values. A version of this exercise for you to try is set out at the end of this chapter.

The exercise can also take the form of a conversation in which employees discuss their favorite books, movies, or music and the reasons why they like those things so much. Learning why someone values their favorite movie is an easy—and fun—way to approach understanding each other's values. Our preferred media often have deeper meanings that describe the morals and life lessons we hold near and dear.

No matter the format you choose, the most important part is showing employees that their values matter—even when they differ from the group.

STEP 2: FACILITATE SPACE FOR TEAM MEMBERS TO SHARE THEIR VALUES

Once team members have identified their own values, managers should create structures for participants to share with one another. This can be as easy as encouraging discussion after the value identification practice. In multiple-day workshops, Mike often runs the "what's your favorite movie" exercise over a dinner where each participant is asked to share the reasons why they chose that particular movie.

But discussions about values should be normalized beyond a one-time workshop. Employees should feel welcome to refer to their own values or the team's collective values in other contexts, like when choosing a difficult course of action. Leaders can model this in the workplace by discussing the values behind their decisions, or asking employees about their own in the course of decision-making.

STEP 3: HIRE FOR SELF-KNOWLEDGE

Another component to this is to hire folks that are self-aware. By doing so, you're ensuring new team members are more likely to be comfortable and capable of sharing their values with others. There are three common tools used by organizations to evaluate a candidate's ability to know themselves. Each can be used to evaluate interviewees on their ability to know themselves, and can be used in conjunction with one another or independently.

The first are psychometric tests, such as the Self-Reflection and Insight Scale (SRIS). The SRIS measures users' ability to participate in self-reflection. Self-reflection is a skill that leads to a wide range of benefits, from higher academic success to lower levels of stress. The SRIS is a common tool, not just in the workplace, but in scientific studies investigating levels of self-reflection in participants.[10,11]

The second tool for evaluating self-reflection is in traditional interview structures. By asking situational questions, particularly follow-up questions to initial responses, hiring managers attempt to gain an understanding of a candidate's self-perspective. In a situational question, an interviewee is asked to tell a story about a past situation, ideally that involved a difficult decision. The key here is to push the candidate beyond their initial response. Why did they act in the way they did? What did they learn from the experience? Given the chance to live that experience again, what would they change? The answers to these secondary questions are a helpful tool to test interviewees for self-awareness and self-reflection.

The third approach uses case-based interview structures. In a case-based interview, the candidate is walked through a hypothetical situation; they're presented with a "case" to solve. This method is used by the top consulting firms to test for structured reasoning ability as well as leadership potential and communication skills. In a values context, the case should focus on making a values-based decision. As the candidate walks through the scenario, the interviewer should test their commitment to the decision ("Are you sure you want to do it that way?") and test why they believe that is the right course of action.

Regardless of the method chosen, it's beneficial to hire individuals who are in touch with their own values. Strong employees can articulate their values and maintain them, even when under pressure.

The Benefits of Sharing

This all sounds good for positive values, you might be thinking, but what about aspects of our character that aren't as attractive? Most folks believe that knowing someone's faults will make you perceive them as less trustworthy, but the opposite is actually true. The more we know the whole person, the deeper our trust for them. This means that the greater the level of sharing among team members, including things that are embarrassing or may come across as weaknesses, the more trust and fluidity there will be in their interactions.[12]

Although much of the research on the topic of vulnerability in the workforce centers on leaders and the utility of leaders being vulnerable, these takeaways are equally applicable in a team context. Vulnerability from any team member can lead to benefits like connection-building, trust, a sense of belonging, and innovation. As leading management theorist on teamwork Patrick Lencioni has said: "Remember, teamwork begins by building trust. And the only way to do that is to overcome our need for invulnerability."[13] By consistently demonstrating best practices, leaders and teammates are not only helping their teams to understand them but allowing their teams to start understanding each other. The more we know each other, the easier it is to act with a sense of shared intention and integrity.

Shared intention in teams, we believe, necessitates some version of getting to know one another beyond the organizational or business goals. This will entail an understanding and respect for the values of our team members—and requires a willingness and ability to share our own values and vulnerabilities. The level of engagement that accompanies a highly functional, high-performance team will also have spill-over effects into our families and our communities[14] as we learn to appreciate—and even expect more of—ourselves and our interactions with others.

Identifying Your Own Values

To try the values exercise for yourself, take a look at the following list of 60 values. Sort these into three categories with about 20 values in each: "important," "very important," and the "most important" (the assumption being that none of these are "not important," but you can disregard any that are less important for you). Once you have done that, look at the *most important* list and choose your top 10, and then whittle that down to a top 3. Take your time (this exercise usually requires at least 20–30 minutes) and use your own definition for these values. If there is a value that is not on this list that is important for you, feel free to add it in.

Just like the 100th birthday exercise in Chapter 15, you may discover something that surprises you about yourself. What does that mean? Also, compare your final list to how you are living your life today—are they aligned? You may even decide to revisit your results over the course of several days so that you can revise and more deeply take in what you have discovered. Better still, share your findings with someone close to you so that you have the experience of expressing your values in a meaningful context, seeing what they think these values say about you, and whether you are living in accordance with them.

60 Values list [15]

Achievement	Community
Adventure	Competency
Authenticity	Contribution
Authority	Creativity
Autonomy	Curiosity
Balance	Determination
Beauty	Equality
Boldness	Equity
Compassion	Fairness
Challenge	Faith
Citizenship	Fame

Family	Pleasure
Friendships	Poise
Fun	Popularity
Growth	Recognition
Happiness	Religion
Honesty	Reputation
Humor	Respect
Influence	Responsibility
Inner Harmony	Security
Justice	Self-Respect
Kindness	Service
Knowledge	Spirituality
Leadership	Stability
Learning	Success
Love	Status
Loyalty	Trustworthiness
Openness	Wealth
Optimism	Wisdom
Peace	Work

PART V

Attention

CHAPTER 19

High Performers Are Focused on the Right Things

"Take up one idea. Make that one idea your life—think of it, dream of it, live on that idea. Let the brain, muscles, nerves, every part of your body, be full of that idea, and just leave every other idea alone. This is the way to success."
—Swami Vivekananada

In 1936, Eiji Toyoda, a recent mechanical engineering graduate, started work at his cousin's manufacturing plant. His cousin was Kiichiro Toyoda, who had created what would later become the Toyota Motor Corp. Kiichiro initially intended to take over his family's mechanical loom business, but lost out on the position to his brother-in-law. Deciding instead to focus on building world-class cars, Kiichiro recruited his cousin Eiji to help with operations. And help he did.

By the 1950s, Eiji had become central to the company's operations. He was hyper-focused on understanding how to scale production while improving quality and efficiency. To understand what it took to be world-class in the field, Eiji visited the Ford Motor Co.'s River Rouge Complex in Dearborn, Michigan.[1] He was astounded by what he saw. While Toyota had produced a total of 2,500 cars in its 13 years of existence, that single Ford plant manufactured 8,000 vehicles per day. Per day! Eiji went back to Japan and turned their tiny car

153

manufacturing operation into what would later become the backbone of the second-largest world economy.

Much of Toyota's success can be attributed to Eiji's unique way of seeing the world. Rather than inventing new ways to approach the factory line, as many competitors did, Eiji paid attention to his workers, searching for ways to increase efficiency. Despite having been on factory floors his entire career—or perhaps because of it— he would note each and every detail of the process. If he saw a worker struggling, he wouldn't intervene with a solution, but observe their reaction in order to collect more data. A worker struggling to fit a seal onto a car door wasn't a singular problem to Eiji; it was a symptom of wider inefficiencies. He wanted to fix these problems at the operations level, not on a case-by-case basis.

By paying attention to his workers, Eiji knew when to be proactive and when to be reactive. His ability to see the patterns in their challenges allowed him to create the Toyota Production System: the manufacturing process so powerful that American car makers began visiting Japan in order to learn it. What Eiji used was a powerful type of paying attention: focusing on one problem (in his case, the optimization of production methods) over a sustained period of time.

Open the Aperture to Focus It

But there's more than one way to pay attention. If you're active in the finance world, you know the story of Dr. Michael Burry, immortalized in the book *The Big Short* by Michael Lewis (and the movie of the same name). Burry was one of the few who predicted the financial crisis in 2008, and he did it by paying attention—but in a different way than Eiji Toyoda. As he detailed in a *New York Times* op-ed, he realized in the early 2000s that a wide set of mortgage-backed securities wasn't as secure as the market thought. He saw that, despite their high ratings from agencies, these financial instruments were built on risky loans to folks who were unlikely to pay them back.[2]

Burry made millions from his observations. His investment firm, Scion Capital, returned almost 500% from its inception in 2000 to Burry's exit in June 2008, and Burry himself is reputed to have made $100 million from his bets on mortgage-backed securities. But this information wasn't exclusive to him. Burry used data that was widely available to anyone at the time—and he didn't start out as a mortgage-backed securities expert. He scanned the market with a broad aperture until he found exploitable imperfections. Then he dug into them. By starting broad and narrowing in on remarkable opportunities, Burry outwitted not only other investors, but the Federal Reserve.

Attention as a Tool

Whether you hone in on your expertise or survey widely for opportunity, the power to pay attention can be the difference between mediocre performance and high performance. Since it can be difficult to conceptualize abstract skills like attention, think of attention as a flashlight in a dark room. Attention allows us to focus on one aspect of reality and ignore all the noise around us. Sometimes we use a broad beam of light, like Burry looking for an investment opportunity, and sometimes we use a very tight one, like Toyoda studying his employees.

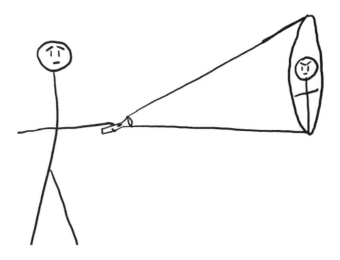

While we often feel like we are the center of the universe, everything that constitutes our existence falls within the small circle of our attention flashlight's scope. Every experience we've ever had and everything we've ever known lies in its miniscule spotlight. Realizing how small that is relative to everything that is happening around us can be a dismaying thought, but it can also be a freeing perspective.

Perhaps most important is the fact that we have a measure of control over that beam in the darkness. Specifically, what we have power over is how much we direct our attentional flashlight. We can let it be dragged around by external forces or we can be intentional and do the directing.

By being intentional about where we shine that light, we are defining our experience of life, and that is an immense power that we should not relinquish lightly. As Epictetus cautioned, "You become what you give your attention to. . . .If you yourself don't choose what thoughts and images you expose yourself to, someone else will."[3]

The difficulty in directing our own flashlight comes down to the severely limited number of things that we can decide to focus on in our lives. When Mike, Sekoul, and Dan were kids, there were only a few television channels, so we only had to choose between three different shows to watch at any one time. The limitations of choice made the decision both easier and harder: we didn't have to wade through thousands of Netflix shows, but our siblings invariably wanted to watch the other channel. With the advent of the internet, we're faced with a new version of this two-pronged problem. On the one hand, we have an infinite set of choices to focus our attention on. On the other hand, every choice we make is curated, tailored for us by whichever algorithm is tracking our consumption patterns.

> 60% of people agree that the abundance of choice in today's digital age makes it more difficult to focus on the right things.

The Illusion of Choice

Many of our choices aren't even choices at all. In marketing, there are many examples of "artificial" choices that give us the impression of options, but which aren't really that different (in fact, they're often a curated set of equally bad options). The marketing goal here is often to keep our attention focused on a limited set of choices so that we're forced to pick one of them. In the 1980s, the Cola Wars were an entirely fictitious debate between Pepsi and Coca-Cola, which drove sales for both products. Folks would proclaim their allegiance to one or the other, and the companies themselves drove the false sense of identity that came with allegiance. You were either a Coke person or a Pepsi person, and you should be willing to defend your side, even fight for it![4]

In many countries, the political choice between "left" and "right" has become so powerful that people are willing to riot, kill, and risk their lives in the name of allegiance to one or the other, regardless of whether the parties have relatively similar policies or not. Realistically, when placed on a spectrum of political thought, many major parties in the Western world aren't really that far apart, creating an illusion of real choice. Your vote for one of the two de facto major parties (such as Republican or Democrat in the United States) would likely perpetuate a governing system that has been relatively unchanged for hundreds of years. This matters because part of being intentionally focused is being wary of how our attention is drawn to concepts that may have no real value or that may not present the full extent of our real options.

> As an exercise, look at your life and see if you can identify any artificial choices that you are choosing between. What are the things that seem like an opportunity to choose between (usually two) options, but that when looked at with a broader perspective, turn out to be fairly similar in the grand scheme of things?

Pepsi and Coke are not the only example of this, and you might be surprised at how many of these illusory choices are all around us. For example, when Mike was coming out of law school, most of his fellow students were deciding whether to be litigators or transactional lawyers, but they were all aiming at the same big corporate firms. Very few were looking at careers in public interest law or even further afield in non-law related jobs like consulting or politics (where many of them eventually wound up). Their attention was artificially focused on a small subset of possibilities and those were the only choices that they could see.

Next we explore the connection between intention and attention. We discuss how you can use attention to nourish your intention as well as use intention to improve your focus. When you look at the high performers you strive to emulate, think about how they control their attention. Odds are, they know how to direct their flashlight in the darkness to shine on what they choose to find valuable.

CHAPTER 20

Directing the Spotlight

"The faculty of voluntarily bringing back a wandering attention, over and over again, is the very root of judgment, character, and will."

—William James

As you read this book, you're doing far more work than you realize. Whether it's fighting your buzzing phone, a chatty child, an overheard conversation, or the persistent gnaw of a recurring thought, you're working to maintain focus. While modern life may leave most of us feeling distracted and scattered, we're doing a much better job of resisting distractions than we give ourselves credit for.

Our ability to filter information is another human superpower. We're constantly exposed to overwhelming amounts of data, both internal and external. Yet our brains are, for the most part, able to execute near-perfect traffic control. Not only do our minds allow us to navigate our environments effectively, but they do so while carrying out endless unconscious functions: maintaining homeostasis, pumping our heart, and digesting our breakfast.

Building a World, One Piece at a Time

When most of us gaze at the words on this page, we're only using about 1–2 degrees of our visual field to gather information.[1] And yet, we have a sense of full visual awareness in most environments.

BUILDING REALITY

Our experience of the world comes down to how we direct these slivers of attention. Consider the Buddhist parable of the blind men and the elephant: a group of blind men have never come across an elephant before.[2] When they do so for the first time, they each feel a different part of the animal and try to describe it. One man feels a tusk and believes the animal to be made of a hard shell. Another touches the trunk and believes the animal is like a thick snake.

In some versions of the story, the ensuing disagreements are resolved peacefully, while in others, the men suspect each other of lying. Just like their differing perceptions of the elephant, our perceptions of the world are drastically impacted by how we focus our attention, and more specifically, what we intentionally choose to pay attention to.

For example, imagine dinner with a friend. You've both been busy, and you're elated to see one another. Soon after you're seated, a group sits at a nearby table—a rowdy bunch, filling the restaurant with loud laughter and obnoxious jokes. You try to stay present with your friend, but neither of you can help glancing over every time the others erupt with laughter. Your time together is quickly being defined by the noisy neighbors, instead of the pleasure of being with each other. The ability to direct our attention and focus on what we want to engage with will make the difference between an enjoyable reunion or an irritating one.

Attention as a Magnet

If you're familiar with distraction, you know that our brains are controlled by more than just top-down intentions. Our attentional spotlight is impacted by anything and everything, from our deepest emotions to a passing thought. We call these distractions, but they're more accurately thought of as attractions. They're our brain's attempt to navigate us safely through our environment—but bottom-up attentional processes can be a burden when they're out of control.

These attractions act like magnets, pulling our attention away from our primary tasks. While we need to make space for curiosity, there are times when we need to buckle down and focus. Let's investigate a few of the most common attentional magnets and how to best navigate them.

MAGNET #1: EMOTIONS

Whether you're processing a major argument or mourning the loss of a pet, negative events and the strong emotions they cause can make it difficult to intentionally direct your attention. This is because negative emotions often serve as signals that something is wrong and should be attended to and our negativity bias makes negative things more attention grabbing than positive ones. Even trivial day-to-day events drastically influence which parts of our surroundings we pay attention to, even beyond the immediate experience.[3] This means that a mild irritation at work might dictate whether the obnoxious neighbors at the table next to us in the restaurant annoy us or not later that evening.

When it comes to emotional states, our attentional spotlight has built-in tracking capabilities. If you're feeling optimistic, you're more likely to notice the good around you—perhaps your colleagues are being extra nice, or you saw an act of random kindness on your way to work. But if you're feeling anxious, you're more likely to notice all the things that could go wrong. Instead of hearing your colleagues' nice words, you're dreading the work for a deliverable due that afternoon. Instead of noticing an act of kindness on the street, you're focused on whether the traffic ahead of you is going to make you even later than you already are. We tend to notice anything that will resonate with our current emotional state, as if those states magnetically lead our attentional spotlight to relevant corners of the room.

Luckily, there are techniques that can help us reduce this effect and stay more intentional. By practicing mindfulness, we can limit how emotions impact our attention and stop zeroing in on negative aspects of the day when we're feeling low. To further develop mindfulness, there are a few simple tricks you can practice.

When you catch yourself noticing negative thought after negative thought, challenge yourself to find three positives before your next negative one. Shift your attention, and your outlook will follow. Another common way to redirect negative emotions is through gratitude practice, an increasingly popular strategy proven to reduce stress and improve mental and physical health. Studies show that regular gratitude practice can reduce symptoms of depression and anxiety, improve sleep, and even lower blood pressure.[4,5] Practicing gratitude can look like gratitude journaling or listing what you're thankful for at the beginning or end of the day. You can even turn to listing reasons for gratitude when you catch yourself in a negative slump, whenever and wherever it might happen.

Try it now; think about three things that you are grateful for at this moment in your life. Dig into each of them—why are you grateful for that thing? What does it bring into your life? Even a quick exercise like this, done regularly, has been shown to have significant impacts on your quality of life and your ability to pay attention to the right things.

> 88% of people believe that practicing gratitude helps improve their ability to focus.

Building on this, and adding in an acceptance practice, Mike asks his kids every night to state the best part of their day and one thing about their day that they accept, even though it might not have been very pleasant.

MAGNET #2: NOVELTY

We've evolved to understand and pay sharp attention to changes in our environment. And for good reason: our attraction to novelty helps us avoid a bus when crossing the street, and leads us to investigate new ideas or environments. Our desire for novelty is strong enough that many companies that want our attention will incorporate novelty in their messages to draw us in. When photographs in the news are more novel—they contain surprising or unusual images—we're more likely to give them our attention.[6]

Most of our surroundings—especially our digital surroundings—are designed to enhance our desire for novelty. Every notification on your phone, buzz, badge, pop-up, or sound, is competing for your attention. In work places, these forms of novelty often act as distractions. To accomplish focused work, we need to eliminate these distractions from our working environments.[7]

Our personal devices are the easiest to redesign. We can simply remove all forms of notifications from our gadgets. But the wider world is harder to restructure. The best we can do is increase our awareness of what draws our attention and why. Are we scrolling through headlines or news feeds that are using novelty gimmicks to win our attention? Does a mindless phone game feel satisfying because of the new rewards you keep unlocking? Instead of letting novelty take control, practice identifying when novelty is contributing to undesirable behaviors. From there, where possible you can intentionally restructure your environment to limit novelty magnets, like leaving electronic devices in another room to stay focused.

MAGNET #3: GOALS

Not all of our attentional magnets begin outside of our control and not all of them are negative. Goal-setting is a way to intentionally direct our attention, even before we fall victim to distraction. Three decades of research on goals has found that they're immensely helpful in guiding our attention toward useful tasks, thereby increasing our performance.[8] Goals are essential for structuring how we use our attention.

Goals don't just redirect our behavior but our cognition. When we're given feedback in a number of areas, we're more likely to improve in the dimensions that align with our goals. A study found that drivers who received input on multiple aspects of their driving only made progress in the areas that they had already had goals for.[9] Beyond shaping our priorities, our goals change the way we interact with the world.

If you don't already have one, create a formal goal-setting process—and not just at work. These goals shouldn't be broad: instead of "get better at driving," goals should lean toward specific outputs or skills. Is parallel parking your weakest link? Do you need to work on smoother cornering? By being specific, you can redirect both your behavior and cognition toward your desired outcomes. If you've clearly defined amazing parallel parking as an actionable goal, you'll start to notice every time you see a perfect execution from another driver. You'll even heighten your perception of your own parking skills—all because you intentionally made a goal to improve.

CHAPTER 21

Spotlights at Work

"To lead people, walk beside them."

—Lao Tzu

In a small, colorless cubicle within a sprawling corporate office sits Brian, an unassuming middle-aged man. For the past two decades, Brian has been the company's most reliable data analyst. His days have revolved around numbers, charts, and spreadsheets: a world he has always found comfort in. But he's also on the company social committee and helps to organize the yearly holiday party and other events.

As he sips his coffee and opens his computer, he notices an important-looking message. Seems to be a new memo from management. They are launching a new initiative, a company-wide race to increase utilization by 25% over the next quarter. The memo is filled with buzzwords like *synergy*, *optimization*, and *growth hacking*. Brian's heart starts racing. He's fuming. He's been trying to tell senior management that blindly looking at utilization without considering employee engagement and retention is a terrible idea. In general, he knows they understand, and he fully supports the company's mission to be the best in its industry. But this message is so tone-deaf. He knows exactly who came up with this terrible idea and has half a mind to march in there right now and tell them what he thinks! Instead, he takes a deep breath, shrugs it off, and does his best to avoid this deluge of stupidity.

Usually he would raise a point at the next town hall. But this time, something's different. There's a sense of disconnect that he can't shake off. The misalignment between management's stated goals and the realities of the business is so significant that it isn't worth a conversation at all. They're focused on blind growth, which would jeopardize relationships with employees, customers, and the very core of the company's purported people-focused values.

Attentional Spotlight: Workplace Edition

In Chapter 20, we look at how our realities are shaped by the fraction of the world we engage with through our attention. While many factors can affect our attentional spotlight, we can exercise some level of control over it, getting better at steering it back toward what matters to us with practice and intention.

Organizations are complex, dynamic systems—they have a multitude of competing priorities. In a sense, they're like a brain. In the same way that the brain prioritizes tasks, many organizations have metrics like Objectives and Key Results (OKRs) or Key Performance Indicators (KPIs) to focus their resources.

KPIs are meant to represent a measure of progress toward the overarching goals that a company wants to reach. These indicators simplify complexity and nuance to create goalposts that are far more transparent and actionable. However, in the same way that our attentional spotlight can drastically alter our perception of reality, an organization's KPIs can completely shift the way it sees the world and approaches its work. For this reason, choosing the right ones to attend to is incredibly important.

KPIs as Shared Intentions

KPIs are more than just a tool for aligning work in an organization. They ideally represent something that matters to us personally—a shared intention. In the same way that we align ourselves with ideas, political parties, and sports teams; we pool our collective will to work on a shared vision within a company. The KPI is the concrete manifestation of that vision—something that has been shown by research even at a neurological level.[1]

Company leaders who want to rally and inspire employees to higher performance need to understand that directives from leadership will be tapping into and affecting the employees' personal drivers. For Brian, it might be a desire for building better communities. For his co-worker Alyssa, it might be a desire to optimize. Whatever their driving forces are, highlighting KPIs that don't reflect those personal drivers are likely to foster disengagement. Unfortunately, most goals set by leaders fall short of meeting what matters most to their employees because, as we see in Chapter 18, most leaders don't understand what their colleagues' values are.

The Problem with Most KPIs
In addition to KPIs (as well as many goals set for us outside of work) being disconnected from what people care about, KPIs are typically disconnected from the ways that people are motivated. Specifically, leaders fail to grasp that individuals have unique motivators. Research on motivation has shown that people tend to fall into one of four "achievement goal orientations." These groups were suggested by Andrew Elliot and Holly McGregor in a classic 2001 paper,[2] and are as follows:

- **Mastery-Approach Group**: Motivated by gaining mastery of a task. "We at Acme Co. strive to be the first to achieve 90% utilization, which we've never achieved before."
- **Performance-Approach Group**: Motivated by performing better than their peers at the task. "We at Acme Co. strive to rank number one in the world on utilization."
- **Mastery-Avoidance Group**: Motivated by not performing worse at the task than before. "We must not drop below our historical low of 72% utilization."
- **Performance-Avoidance Group**: Motivated to avoid looking incompetent or worse than others at the task. "We cannot fall behind the industry standard of 70% utilization."

Research shows that while people may be motivated by factors from other groups, they tend to have a dominant group they belong to, which stays fairly stable over time. Motivating people is therefore not only about understanding human psychology generally but about understanding the psychology of each individual.

Understanding that people have unique motivators that can change over time can help us to understand why KPIs fail to motivate most of them. For example, if I set KPIs that assume everyone wants to gain mastery, then I'm probably not connecting very well with people who are focused on not looking incompetent. These factors can also help us reframe what might otherwise look like poor performance. For example, Andrew Howell and David Watson[3] showed that while procrastination is typically treated as an issue with self-regulation, it is actually associated with the Mastery-Avoidance group—being motivated by not performing worse at the task than before. In a separate study, Huanhuan Wang and James Lehman[4] showed that personalized motivational feedback that was tied to a person's achievement goal orientation can improve learning.

> As an exercise, take a few minutes and imagine (whether you are a leader or not) that you had to set KPIs for a few of your colleagues that would help motivate them at work. If their motivation was your primary goal, what KPIs would you create for each of them? Have fun with this—imagine that there are no limits or constraints on what these could be. What did you come up with? What does that tell you about what you think motivates the folks you work with? Now let's add back in overall organizational goals—how could you create a set of KPIs that both motivates the individuals and helps increase their performance in a way that supports the organization's objectives?

What are the implications of this research? For one, if we want people in an organization to pay attention to the right things, then we must start understanding what motivates them and then give them clear goals that are personalized and aligned with their actual motivations. Often, this means creating broader organizational goals and KPIs that are meant to inspire, not organize, and then cascading these down into more tactical measures for smaller teams and at the individual level, so that we can target the motivations of those people and the groups they belong to.

Let's come back to Brian. The reason he's irritated with that memo isn't necessarily because he disagrees that utilization is important. He may fully agree but might also believe that the best way to do that is by increasing employee engagement—something that isn't called out in the memo. What might have been more effective for him is a memo that calls out a core goal and then lists important pillars supporting that goal. Pillars allow people like Brian to see themselves in, and rally behind, the core goal. And then letting Brian's manager create a set of goals just for Brian that are expressed in a way that taps into what he cares about, but that still support the broader organizational goals. In other words, organizational goals are opportunities to shine a broad spotlight, but that light should be narrowed to highlight the goals of the audience, not the goals of those who drafted the KPIs.

> 80% of people agree that having a clear connection between their personal goals and their organization's goals is important for them to feel engaged.

A KPI is not an objective statement of what's important—it's a motivational (or demotivational) tool and should be treated as such. It functions as an attentional spotlight—and just like we must use those deliberately at an individual level, it's important to use them effectively at a group level. Doing so will not only improve performance in an organization, but individuals who feel their motivations being met and attended to will feel more engaged and supported. Shared intention, as we have seen, is one of the most powerful forces we have, and leaders who understand this more fully will be able to meet all individuals in the organization in ways that are deeply motivating.

CHAPTER 22

Intentional Wandering

"You must have chaos within you to give birth to a dancing star."

—Friedrich Nietzsche

Most of our discussion thus far has been centered on how to use proactive attention—choosing what to focus on and following through. In this chapter, we explore the other side of the equation: how can we use reactive attention to develop and support our intention? In common parlance, we often say our attention is drawn to something. Yes, most of the time this can be distracting, but being reactive to stimuli—even random interruptions—can also be beneficial, even game-changing, as new inputs potentially alter our perspective with significant insights. Just like Archimedes in the bathtub or Newton with his apple, eureka moments sometimes come from unexpected sources.

The Benefits of a Wandering Mind
In the world of psychology, proactive and reactive attention are more often referred to as *top-down* and *bottom-up* attention, respectively. While they're both clearly important, bottom-up attention alerts us to the unexpected, the new. For our ancestors, that may have meant a life-threatening event like a poisonous snake on the path—it was reactive attention that allowed them to quickly change course of

action. But reactive attention can be applied to distractions that go beyond physical survival, such as an unexpected idea popping into our heads.

And unlike a poisonous snake at our feet, unexpected stimuli aren't all bad. The ideas that pop into our heads are the result of our unconscious at work, making connections our conscious minds might not have access to. A study from Northwestern University found that people who scored high on creative achievement did a worse job at filtering out "noise" than those who scored lower.[1] This was due to their "leaky" censoring gating—a tendency to let more stimuli into their field of consciousness. This means that if you're more likely to get distracted by a barking dog or a runaway thought, you're more likely to come up with unusual, "out of the box" perspectives and score higher on measures of creativity.[2]

Structuring Your Environment

Our challenge in positively harnessing our attention is that we may not know how to best optimize our proactive and reactive attention—or we may not even know that we have the ability to significantly improve how we work with our attention. As it turns out, the most powerful tool for attention we have at our disposal is our ability to change our environment so that only the useful "noise" gets through to us. At The Decision Lab, choice architecture is one of the most important things we work on, which includes structuring environments for improved, optimized focus. We first apply behavioral science principles to better understand how people make their decisions—then, perhaps in tandem with other interventions, we help them make better decisions by restructuring their environments.

A key principle of choice architecture is that controlling our actions and attention is difficult, but changing our environment is relatively easy. Since leaky attention begets creativity if the inputs are the rights ones, we can create environments where our attention "leaks" productively.

The strategy to change our environment, rather than our natural inclination, has been around for centuries. Perhaps the most dramatic example of choice architecture comes from Greek literature. In Homer's *Odyssey*, Odysseus, the king of Ithaca, is returning home from the Trojan

War a hero, but he has to pass the Island of Sirens, known for luring men to their death. In order to safely hear the Sirens' beautiful songs as his ship passed by the island, Odysseus is taught by the sorceress Circe to make his men plug their ears with wax and tie him to the mast. Making sure that the crew cannot hear the songs, and allowing Odysseus to hear the music but unable to act on his resultant overpowering desire to jump into the ocean. Note here that Odysseus makes clear choices about who gets to be distracted by what—with the help of his crew, he creates an environment where he can reap the benefits of listening to the beautiful music without the negative consequences.

While we might not be facing enchanting Sirens, nor does our behavioral science firm advise our clients to tie themselves to the mast and plug their ears with wax, we can take after Odysseus's admirable ability to restructure his environment. Nowadays, for example, many people choose to keep their cell phones outside of their bedroom at night to overcome the temptation to fire off late-night emails or check social media after bedtime. As we set intentions for how we will best use our time, we should be mindful to plan ahead for potential interruptions, and set ourselves up for success early on—not after we hear the bewitching sound of the Sirens' songs (or the ping of a new message on our phone). As experts have found, the keys to focusing in heavily distracted environments are the ability to set rules for yourself and stick to them, and intentionally altering our surroundings to decrease the effects of potential derailers.

One simple way to put this in practice for yourself: when you are working on a focused task, like reading this book, keep a piece of paper (ideally not your phone or another electronic tool) close by. Whenever an errant thought pops into your mind, write it down without thinking about it too much. When you're done with your task (or are taking a break) review your notes and see if there is anything valuable in there. This will help you to diminish the effect of distracting thoughts but may also help you to find some interesting tangents that you might not have otherwise noticed if you were focused on suppressing the ideas that pop into your mind.

Reframing Your Language and Story

Choice architecture can also involve changes in our internal environment, for example, how we phrase things as well as the stories we tell ourselves about who we are (or are not). In dieting, for example, the concept of a "cheat day" can be seen as a change in our internal frame for our diet, effectively reconfiguring our concept of dieting.

Interestingly, cheat days have not yet been shown to have significant beneficial effects from a metabolic or caloric perspective (there are some studies that show that it is helpful in replenishing leptin, which helps us to judge when we're full, but those effects are usually very short lived and don't really matter in a metabolic sense).[3] But there are significant psychological benefits to allowing yourself to be, in effect, distracted from your primary goal by gorging yourself on foods that you would not otherwise allow yourself to eat. First of all, you satisfy your cravings, and knowing that you have this opportunity to do so makes the days where you are not "cheating" easier to tolerate. Furthermore, people tend to overdo it on their cheat day, making themselves feel sick or less energetic than usual, and thus, reinforcing the benefit of their otherwise healthy lifestyle through a negative reward trigger. But perhaps most interesting for our purposes, recent research has shown that by conceiving of our "cheat day" as a "treat day" instead and seeing the eating of things like chocolate cake as an uncommon celebration (as opposed to a source of guilt), we lead ourselves to healthier eating more regularly.[4]

So giving in to temptation in a controlled way, even when it runs against our overall intention in the short term, can be beneficial in the long term if we're thoughtful (and intentional) about how, when, and what we give in to that temptation with. And it is in this interplay, of background and foreground, that we can be truly high performing.

The Stories We Tell

Perhaps the most important aspect to aligning our reactive focus with our intentions is around the stories we tell about ourselves. In a direct sense, this is a matter of restructuring our internal environment. As we get better at setting and attending to our intentions, we should be creating a new way of thinking about ourselves that aligns with those intentions, creating coherence between our behavior and our mindset. If I want to be a more well-read person, the more I tell myself that I am a person who reads a lot, and the more I share that identity with others, the easier it becomes to do the things that are necessary to achieve that goal.

This way, our intentions work in the background as a sort of underlying guide, rather than us always having to do the hard work of keeping them in the forefront of our minds. Work by Albert Bandura[5] and Carol Dweck,[6] which have become very popular, highlight the effect that how we talk and think about ourselves can have on our ability to always act in accordance with our intentions. Sometimes simple changes can make a huge difference. For example, Dweck's insight around growth mindset revolves around the idea that rather than saying "I'm not good at this. . ." we say "I'm not good at this, *yet*. . .". By making this small change, we release preconceived limits that we've placed on ourselves.

Open Expectations Lead to Unexpected Paths

Last, as we've seen, intentions can and should change over time. By allowing yourself to be open to the right amount of distraction, you create the space for new ideas or new intentions to arise. Perhaps the thing that draws your attention away from your current goal is actually drawing your attention to something that will form the basis for your next goal.

Cecilia Payne-Gaposchkin is a wonderful example of the power and utility of distraction. While focusing on botany at Cambridge, Payne-Gaposchkin got a free ticket to a lecture by an astronomer, Sir Arthur Eddington, when someone else had to drop out. After the lecture, she was so excited by what she had heard that she ran home and wrote out almost the whole lecture verbatim. By attending the lecture, she had allowed her mind to wander outside her current goals—and was pleasantly surprised. Following that revelatory moment, Payne-Gaposchikin abandoned botany as her main focus and turned her attention to physics and astronomy. She turned out to be one of the 20th century's most important astronomers, discovering, among other things, the chemical composition of stars and stellar temperatures.

Our takeaway here is that while focused attention is a key to living your intentions, allowing yourself to be distracted in an intentional way is also a crucial ingredient to high performance. In fact, if we do not cultivate the capacity for allowing our attention to wander productively, we may miss the opportunity to be inspired by something new that may ignite a whole new passion. So go find that astronomy lecture for yourself!

CHAPTER 23

Not All Flow Is Created Equal

"I had worked hard for nearly two years, for the sole purpose of infusing life into an inanimate body. . . .I seemed to have lost all soul or sensation but for this one pursuit."
—Mary Shelley, *Frankenstein*

For Lila, her downtown studio has always been her escape. A sanctuary that protects her from the hustle and bustle of the outside world. A magical place where the combination of pigments and canvas become worlds in their own right, worlds that she creates and then becomes enveloped in. As she steps into the studio early this Saturday morning, Lila feels more excited than usual. There's a burning anticipation in the pit of her stomach. An idea has been simmering in her mind for the last few days, and when she woke up this morning, it had suddenly crystalized.

As she enters the studio, she removes her sneakers and steps onto the paint-splattered hardwood floor, making her way to the sunlit corner where an empty canvas is waiting. A subtle smile makes its way across her face as she sits down and grabs a brush. She takes out a large tube of cobalt paint, squeezes it and watches a blob ooze onto her palette. She continues with several other tubes and mixes the perfect shade of teal. She dabs her brush on the paint and her world dissolves as she paints her morning vision.

She applies color after color, following the vision and letting it guide her hands. Streaks of cerulean followed by whispers of white make their way across the canvas. After what seems like just a few minutes, she looks up and realizes the sun is beginning to set, casting long shadows on the studio floor. Lila glances at the canvas and realizes that a painting that captures what she saw that morning has materialized where there was only blank canvas before. She looks through the window and sees a neon pizza sign turn on across the street. Her stomach gurgles, and she suddenly realizes she's starving. Time to step back into her other life and eat some food.

Is Flow the End-All-Be-All?

Most of us have experienced what psychologists call "flow" at some time or other in our lives. It's been described in many ways, perhaps most common as being "in the zone." Mihály Csíkszentmihályi first introduced the concept of flow in 1975, and it has now risen in popularity decades after his initial research—becoming a very trendy topic in management and personal efficacy literature.[1] One potential explanation for the revival is the quickening pace of society. The number of distractions we have to deal with has become almost unbearable, and flow seems like a perfect antidote.

In the world of flow, distractions act like thieves of agency that steal moments of attention from us, making it harder for us to achieve our goals. Flow is seen as the ultimate expression of agency—an experience of pure, undivided attention. A bulletproof mental state. Except it's not all that it is purported to be. As we'll explore in this chapter, the truth is actually a little more nuanced than that. And flow is better thought of as a tool than as an end goal. A tool to use mindfully in order to express our intentions.

How Does Flow Work?

In "Flow Theory and Research," Csíkszentmihályi argues that two conditions must be met to achieve a flow state.[2] First, we must be engaged in an activity that feels challenging, but not overly so. The activity must push us just outside of our comfort zone but not to the point of feeling stuck or utterly incompetent. If something is too easy, our minds will wander and leave us bored. If something is too difficult, we will end up feeling anxious and immobilized. Second, the activity must have clear goals and immediate feedback. This allows us to more tightly engage with the activity, monitoring how our actions change the result and creating a strong sense of agency.

If these two prerequisites are met, Csíkszentmihályi continues, then we may enter the flow state, which is characterized by the following six conditions:

- ◆ Focused concentration in the present moment.
- ◆ Merging action and awareness.
- ◆ Loss of reflective self-consciousness.
- ◆ A sense of control over our actions.
- ◆ Distortion of time.
- ◆ Experience of the activity as intrinsically rewarding.

Csíkszentmihályi began his research studying people like Lila. As he looked around at various levels of engagement at work, he realized that artists and athletes would go to extreme lengths when they were fully absorbed in their work.[3] Many painters would continue for long stretches of time without eating or sleeping, almost as if they were entranced. All of this sounds great, especially since our brains have a mechanism that can make hard work effortless when we are in a flow state. Like an autopilot that allows us to achieve Herculean tasks that might feel impossible if we really thought about them.

But there is a problem with flow. Research has shown that flow can be dangerous for the very reason it's so appealing: it's an intrinsically motivating experience. This means that the experience of flow can feel addictive regardless of the task that produces it.

Not All Flow Is Created Equal

While being in a flow state is more enjoyable than feeling distracted, not all flow is created equal. In fact, perhaps surprisingly, not all flow is beneficial. As far back as 2008, Andrew Thatcher and colleague showed that the same experiences we describe as flow exist in both desirable and undesirable states.[4] In a study of 1,399 people, they showed that measures of flow correlate with feelings of procrastination on the internet. The same construct that Csíkszentmihályi describes as productive can, if we engage in it unintentionally, lead to mindless scrolling. The key point here is (again) intention—we need to make conscious choices about what we allow to engage us in flow states and how we use these moments.

But there is more to it. Just as flow might lead to lower productivity like mindless internet scrolling, flow can also lead to antisocial behavior. In 2008, Yuval Noah Harari (of best-selling *Sapiens* fame) published a paper called "Combat Flow: Military, Political, and Ethical Dimensions of Subjective Well-Being in War."[5] In it, Harari discusses how combat situations can often create the perfect circumstances for flow. In the words of an American soldier he quotes: "I felt a drunken elation. . . I had never experienced anything like it before. When the line wheeled and charged across the clearing, the enemy bullets whining past them, wheeled and charged almost with drill-field precision, an ache as profound as the ache of orgasm passed through me."[6] Harari suggests that flow isn't necessarily a state of subjective well-being, but rather a state of abstraction from well-being to achieve an important task. This is a subtle difference, but it makes sense from an evolutionary point of view—we evolved to be useful and survive, not to be happy. It's wise to apply a critical eye to anything that feels too good to be true, biologically speaking, and to make sure that we're using our flow states in the service of things that are good for us.

Just ask Mike Dixon and his colleagues, who studied the "dark flow" of gambling.[7] They found that casino slot machines have, intentionally or not, created a near-perfect flow experience by fulfilling the two prerequisites: the right level of challenge, and clear goals with immediate feedback. And as our understanding of flow has become more sophisticated, so have the tools developed to keep us in these states. A recent addition to slot machines is a mechanism that facilitates flow called a "loss disguised as a win" (LDW). An LDW occurs when a player bets a certain amount and "wins" a smaller amount—like betting 25 cents and winning 20 cents back. Although this interaction is a loss, the partial "win" creates a smoother experience for the gambler by giving them a form of immediate positive feedback. Their brain perceives the loss as a win, despite the math, helping the gambler feel competent despite obvious evidence to the contrary.

Because flow feels good, the experience of flow can be used as a tool by those who are trying to engage our attention. In scenarios like gambling, flow isn't just pleasant—it is purposefully being used to add an additional layer of addiction. Dixon found that dark flow is correlated with higher scores on depression scales as well as a higher reported subjective well-being while gambling. The highs are higher, but the lows are dangerously low. Clearly, flow is far more nuanced than its mainstream perception.

The Intentional Flow Spectrum

In his original work, Csíkszentmihályi describes a type of flow that provides a strong sense of competence and agency. But examples like gambling show us that these feelings can be misleading. While gamblers may experience a higher *feeling* of agency, they're actually put in a situation where they have less self-control over their actions. The addictive nature of the flow state can push us toward activities that don't actually align with our goals.

The picture of flow in the mainstream media misses its dual nature. More often than not, flow is characterized as a very immediate application of agency toward the achievement of some goals. But this picture-perfect conception of flow often forgets about the time horizon of these goals. Our short-term goals, like winning a hand of poker, might be in opposition to our long-term goals, like saving for a house. Flow is only helpful to us if, like Lila, our flow-inducing actions align with our long-term intentions.

Think about flow in your own life. Perhaps you feel flow when you're completing a task for work that you want to check off your list. But how much does it matter to you whether that task is actually aligned with your broader values and goals? Could it be that flow is sometimes used as a way to mask the uselessness of activities? Probably. We need to be critical of flow-inducing activities and assess how they align with our goals. Intrinsic motivation can be the key to our success but also the force that sucks us into our phones for too long. To illustrate this point, let's look at the Intentional Flow Spectrum.

On one end, we have unintentional flow—getting absorbed in stupid stuff. On the other end, there's intentional flow—the ability to channel flow toward something that helps us achieve our long-term goals. The two might feel similar while you're in them, but that's exactly why we must be vigilant when tasks bring us to flow states—because, as we saw earlier, flow is a suspension of critical thinking.

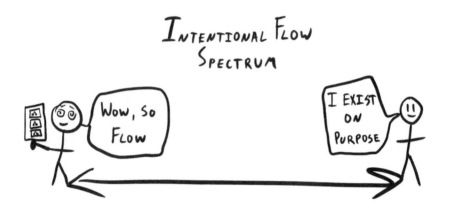

Flowing Our Way to Burnout

Many turn to flow states to overcome burnout. They're not wrong to do so—there's a wealth of research showing that experiences of flow can protect us from burning out.[8] While this should be good news, there's a bit of nuance to these findings. While most evidence links flow to lower burnout symptoms, the opposite can also be true. As Fabienne Aust and her colleagues have found: "The positive associations may indicate that flow experience is potentially addictive and could thus lead to a form of workaholism, which in turn is associated positively with burnout symptoms."[9] In other words, flow can actually lead us to expend incredible amounts of energy and sometimes even push us past our healthy limits. The difference, we contend, is in the extent to which the activity that induces flow is aligned with our broader goals (which should probably include avoiding burning out).

Let's keep in mind that obsessive feelings often come with two sides. If you don't experience flow all that often, you can likely recall the feeling of passion—a close cousin to flow. Passion can make us feel elated, but it comes in two distinct flavors: harmonious passion and obsessive passion.[10] While they might feel the same, they have drastically different consequences. While the former is good, the latter can damage our psychological well-being. Too much obsessive passion can even lead to a crash, just like obsessive flow.

So, we don't benefit from just any flow—we benefit from intentional, goal-aligned, sustainable flow. High performance is the ability to partake in flow-inducing activities that serve our long-term goals, not just make us feel good.

Creating Team Flow

Flow is inherently a psychological state—it describes how we experience the world. Like other psychological states, as Larraitz Zumeta and colleagues have shown,[11] flow can be socially reinforced and shared by multiple people. In the same way we can come together to act on shared intention, we can collectively enter a state of flow. But just like individual flow, we face the same double-edged sword. Flow could mean a team of surgeons working cohesively to save a life, but it could also mean a team of AI researchers working tirelessly to build the AI that ends humanity. Yikes.

So how can we build intentional flow in a team?

Positive psychologists Jef van den Hout and Orin Davis[12] argue that, as opposed to the two prerequisites of individual flow suggested earlier by Csíkszentmihályi, team flow has seven prerequisites:

1. **Collective ambition:** we all strive for the same thing.
2. **Audacious team goal:** that thing we're striving for is known to us all and is tough to achieve.
3. **Open communication:** we speak openly with each other.
4. **Aligned personal goals:** achieving our collective goal also helps each of us individually in some way.
5. **High skill integration:** to achieve our collective goal, we all need to use our skills.
6. **Safety:** we feel relatively safe striving for the team goal.
7. **Mutual commitment:** we all know that each of us is committed.

If these prerequisites are met, then a team is more likely to experience team flow, characterized by a sense of unity, joint progress, mutual trust, and holistic focus. This kind of state is what makes teams so different from each other. Notably, the team flow framework from van den Hout and Davis not only differs from the classic definition of individual flow but also (perhaps inadvertently) describes a more intentional type of flow, where activities aren't just engaging but are also fulfilling.

As you see, *shared intention*, or what the researchers term *collective ambition*, is the primary prerequisite for the establishment of team flow. The rest of the characteristics and prerequisites stem from each of the team members adopting that intention, feeling a sense of togetherness, and as with individual flow, ensuring that what is being asked of each of them aligns with their abilities and interests.

The bottom line is that, as individuals and as teams, we need to be wary of using flow as an escape hatch. While flow can give us momentary bliss, the experience of flow is fundamentally nothing more than a tool we can and should use intentionally to get things done. It is a means to an end rather than the end in itself. As we seek flow states and the benefits they bring, we need to remain mindful of the fact that affirming a stronger sense of agency in our lives, as both individuals and teams, requires us to be more critical of flow and more mindful of the goals we rally around. Intention matters.

CHAPTER 24

Focusing Teams

"Teamwork is the fuel that allows common people to attain uncommon results."

—Andrew Carnegie

Becoming masters of our own attention is one thing, but creating an attentive team is a whole new game. There's only so much we can do to focus the attention of others. Instead of attempts to micromanage our team members, we need to create an environment that sets them up for success and supports that flow-like state where a team can surpass itself and become truly greater than the sum of its parts. But that's hard. In our survey, almost three-fourths of the respondents said that they had never experienced flow as part of a team. It is up to us all as team members and team leaders to create the environments where this is possible.

> 73% of people report having never experienced flow in a team setting.

One summer, Mike worked at Kijiji, a Canadian online classifieds startup owned by eBay. Having worked mostly in law before then, Mike was surprised at how much disagreement there was within the product team he worked on. After a tough meeting, where Mike's ideas were roundly challenged—with one particular team member vehemently questioning his approach—Mike took action. He asked his boss, Andrew, if he or the team member could be moved to another group. Or at least maybe Andrew could have a word with his opponent about the severity of his objections. Andrew responded that a move was out of the question and that he was not going to reprimand the team member. He asked Mike, "Didn't your idea get better because of his challenges? Didn't he force you to dig into a level of detail that you might not otherwise have gone to?" Obviously, it had. The valuable lesson that Mike learned that day was that one must silence one's enemies more underhandedly. . . no, the lesson was that conflict and challenge can be incredibly useful, especially if they drive greater focus. Dissent can help to focus our collective attention.

Nothing Focuses You Like a Fight

Think back to the last time you were in or a witness to a disagreement at work. How did that disagreement change the amount of attention you were paying to what was going on? A funny thing happens during a team kerfuffle. All of a sudden, the team's focus shifts. While this often feels like going off-track (hence Mike's irritation), it can be a beneficial practice. In addition to the benefits we see in Chapter 18, one of the mechanisms through which dissent creates better team decision-making is by pushing people to pay more attention to details.[1] When Mike's colleague pushed back, it forced Mike to dive deeper into his original ideas in order to prove their worth. This is because dissent pushes teams to be more creative—turning even the most passive of participants into active listeners, scrutinizing details from brand-new angles.[2] Perhaps this point deserves further emphasis: dissent between team members *engages everyone more deeply*. Extreme situations, like a heated meeting, may make our blood boil, but these exchanges can boost our team performance if done right.

How does this help us to focus our teams? For one thing, it demonstrates that some level of challenge and adversity is beneficial for team focus. What research shows is that teams that alternate between agreement and disagreement and who also ultimately aim for alignment over consensus perform better than ones where disagreement is frowned on and consensus is a continuous goal. Now let's look at a simple tool that can help to ensure that all team members are aligned on what they are trying to achieve—the 1-2-3 model.

Breaking It Down with the 1-2-3 Model

In case you missed the memo, humans struggle to focus on more than one thing at a time.[3,4] But that doesn't seem to stop us from overloading team members with multiple organizational challenges and tasks to accomplish at once. When inundated with too many tasks, we can easily forget the big picture. So how can we keep team members focused on their duties, and simultaneously cognizant of the wider collective intention?

A simple framework that can help maintain this balance is what we call the 1-2-3 model. Each team member should know the *1 (one) overall organizational goal*, the *2 (two) main duties* of their part of the organization, and the *3 (three) tasks* that they are individually responsible for achieving in the short-to-medium term. Obviously, these six items should be connected to each other, so that the three support the two, and all of these are in service to the overarching goal. The 1-2-3 model is designed to correct the flaw in modern organizations that pushes team members to focus too much attention on their own challenges all the while feeling more disconnected from what the organization is trying to achieve, thus losing sight of the forest for the trees.

For example, imagine a goalkeeper on a soccer team playing an important game. What is their job? Most of us would say that the goalie's job is to stop balls from going in the goal. But the reality is much more complex. The overarching objective of every member of the team, including the goalie, is to win the game. It's worth stopping for a second and focusing on that as everything else is secondary to that goal of winning the game. That's the goalie's *1 organizational goal*. The *2 main duties* of the defense, which includes the goalie, is to help produce plays and to defend against the opponent. Good goalies balance these two roles, coming out to advance plays and also breaking up the opponent's attack. Last, the goalie has *3 tasks* at any moment: (a) they must clear the ball down the field when it comes into their possession; (b) they also have to communicate play production to the team, as from a goalie's unique viewpoint where the goalie can see how the opposing team is reacting to attacks;

and (c) they have to attend to their most fundamental role: to stop balls from going in the goal. As in other types of organizations, to limit the goalie's role to just the last aspect is to miss out on their contribution across the game. Some goalies even add a bonus role. Take Rogerio Céni—he's the professional goalkeeper who has scored the most goals in history, having scored 131 in his career!

Let's put this simple model into practice with a short exercise. Take a moment and ask yourself, do I know what my 1-2-3 is? Do the teams I am on know these for themselves? Try it out right now:

1. What is the *1 organizational goal* that you are helping to work toward? Don't just parrot back a company mission statement here, but really think about what it is that you are working for in the greater scheme of things for the organization. Is it making a profit for shareholders? Is it a broader objective of serving a segment of your community? What is the one thing that everyone who contributes to the organization is helping to achieve?

2. What are your *2 main duties* as part of your organization? If you could describe what it is that you should be spending your time doing in two broad categories, what would these be? As an HR professional, Mike sees his two main tasks as ensuring that the right people are doing the right things and maintaining a supportive company culture. Everything he does can fall into one or the other of these two broad activities.

3. Last, what are the *3 tasks* that you are most responsible for? This is not about objectives, but rather short to medium-term things that you do on a day-to-day basis that make up the components of your duties and are in service to the overarching objective that you are helping to fulfill.

Asking yourself what your 1-2-3s are can help provide clarity, alignment, and focus. Clearly, this is a simplification of the complex roles and responsibilities that we each have in our organizational lives, but doing this exercise will ideally force you to look beyond the minutiae of your role and understand a bit more what it is that you are and should be focused on. This is also a useful exercise to take to your teams, building the alignment necessary for team high-performance.

Create Open Pathways

Although it may seem obvious on the surface, all team members require access to relevant information. Not only does management need to ensure that top-down information sharing is effective, but managers should also be putting the conditions in place for all team members to share information with each other. Studies show that when a workplace is structured to encourage information-sharing— creating a culture of openness and collaboration—then team members are more likely to actively participate in group decisions.[5] To create a collaborative culture, members need to feel motivated to share information. Leaders can work toward this goal by diminishing status differences, increasing group cohesion, and boosting accountability.

Focusing team attention and creating conditions for positive flow increases the likelihood of a highly intentional work environment that aligns personal and organizational goals. We might all have our own flashlights of attention, but when we shine them together in the same direction, we get a lot more light. Guiding the attention of our team members doesn't need to look like authoritarian surveillance— it's as simple as actively blending focused collaboration and dissent in ways that empower team members to do their best.

PART VI

Habits

CHAPTER 25

The Roots of High Performance

"Man's habits are truly more powerful than his deeds."
—Rabindranath Tagore

Sister Madonna Buder was born in St. Louis, Missouri on July 24, 1930. The eldest of three siblings, Buder's parents raised her with a strong sense of discipline and Catholic values, which led her to dedicate her early life to the Church. In her autobiography, *The Grace to Race*, Buder says that even as a teenage equestrian and amateur actress, she had a secret plan to devote her life to the Church.

And so she did, spending much of her life in a Catholic convent. She was a model nun throughout. When she was 48, a priest named Father John suggested she take a run on the beach, telling her that training her body could be a way to improve her mental well-being and become an even better servant to god. Buder found a pair of old shorts and sneakers in a pile of donated clothes and went for a run. And she never stopped.

She began applying the same discipline that she had nurtured in her service to the Church to physical training. Building on her already well-structured and habitual life in the convent, Buder started to intentionally focus on her physical strength and endurance in order to achieve her goals. Her routine was simple: wake up early, swim, bike, and run. However, as simple as the input was, the outcome was nothing short of miraculous.

Sister Buder is, at the time of writing, the oldest person to have ever finished an Ironman Triathlon. The race consists of a 2.4-mile (3.9-km) swim, 112-mile (180-km) bike ride, and a 26-mile (42-km) run. She did it at the age of 82. Since doing her first triathlon at age 52, she's completed more than 340 triathlons and 45 Ironman races. She has defied all odds, overcome dozens of broken bones, and persevered.

While Sister Buder is known as a prime example of starting later in life—as exemplified in a 2016 Nike campaign that highlights her accomplishments—she's also a poster child for habits. And we're not just talking about her outfit. She became an extraordinary athlete with a simple routine, benefiting from the compounding effects of repeated application of intention. Her dedication to long-term habit reinforcement is just as, if not more, remarkable than her age. As she put it herself: "I train religiously."

Our habits are our defining characteristics. They're how the rest of the world perceives us, and they determine how we spend our lives.

There are plenty of great books about the transformative nature of habit formation (James Clear's *Atomic Habits* and Charles Duhigg's *The Power of Habit* are our favorites). But, here, we want to focus on the necessity of habits in realizing your intentions.

The Basics of Deliberate Habits

No matter how present in the moment we might try to be, we're all destined to fill our lives with habits. Our brains don't have enough computing power to make it through a typical day without relying on habitual practices, like brushing our teeth or grabbing our keys on our way out the door. By putting regular tasks on autopilot, we shift our focus to aspects of our lives that require more attention. And that's a good thing! As previously noted, paying attention is a super-power, and doing so with intention helps us maximize our chances of success and high performance.

Habits themselves are neither good nor bad. A nightly flossing ritual is just as much of a habit as a morning cigarette with a cup of coffee. Like everything else, our intentions determine the usefulness of our habits. And just like intention relies on habits, successful habits rely on intention.

There are two steps to intentional habits. The first is their formation. What are you gaining from your repeated actions? Say you take a walk to get ice cream with your family after dinner on Fridays. Sure, the sugar might not fit your goal of reducing processed foods. But you might value the tradition, and the quality family time, over the extra junk food in your system, so that's a habit that might be worth keeping.

The second is re-evaluation. Just like our beliefs, we want to ensure that our habits aren't relics of times gone by. If you're starting to worry about cognitive decline and decide to try challenging your brain more, perhaps doing the crossword during your morning commute on the train would be better than reading trashy fiction? The habits we make for ourselves today won't necessarily be the habits we strive for in five years' time, and a constant re-evaluation is a good ingredient to long-term success.

While forming and re-evaluating your habits, consider both sides of the coin: habits can be actions we do, or they can be actions we avoid. Take an example from the bestselling habit guru himself: James Clear. While Clear no doubt constitutes a high performer, he's prone to bad habits like everyone else. While beginning to write his book, *Atomic Habits*, he foresaw that checking social media on his phone could potentially waste hundreds of hours in the upcoming year.[1] Instead of a futile attempt to white-knuckle his way out of a bad habit, Clear simply automated his behavior. He asked his assistant to change the passwords to his social media accounts every Monday morning, only giving him the logins on Friday evening. Clear automated his decision-making process by eliminating his access to a negative habit. But the best part? He looked ahead to the potential consequences of his habits—and he intentionally took control of them before they could take control of him. Just like Odysseus, who is mentioned in Chapter 22, Clear, in effect, lashed himself to the mast to not be tempted by the Siren song of social media.

Habits as Tools for Intention

Think of intention as a starting point and habits as the follow-through. We intend to accomplish far more than we actually succeed in. Maybe it's our intention to exercise later in the day, or the nagging thought to call an old friend whom we haven't spoken with in too long.

Intention is nearly useless without follow-through—and follow-through, at least in the long term, is nearly impossible without intentional habits.

While it's easy to deliberately complete an action once, or maybe even five times, doing it 5,000 times is hard. Habits require some degree of automation in order to be successful.

We may not all be able to complete an Ironman Triathlon at the age of 82, but we can all get better at using habits to support our intentions, and vice versa. In this section, we dig into how intention and habits can work together to change our lives. As Mahatma Gandhi's old adage goes, "Your actions become your habits, your habits become your values, your values become your destiny."

CHAPTER 26

Taking Control of Unconscious Actions

"Habits are at first cobwebs, then cables."

——Spanish Proverb

Habits are a surprisingly large part of our lives. In the early 2000s,[1] influential psychologist Wendy Wood set out to understand just how much we rely on them. Her team conducted a diary study, asking participants to provide hourly reports of what they did over the course of several days. Across two separate studies like this, Wood and her colleagues showed that about 40% of the activities people reported were habits—actions that participants did on a regular basis without much thought. Habits determine our lives.

How we set up the 40% of our lives that we live habitually can change us profoundly—without us even noticing. The habits may be small, but the consistency that defines them is one of the most powerful forces in our lives. Any financial planner will sing you the praises of compounding interest. Its power comes from a simple principle: even a tiny amount of change each day adds up significantly over time.

Imagine two people, Ada and Mira. They both want to get better at archery but don't have much time. Ada decides she's too busy to take it on this year, so she'll start her archery training on her sabbatical next year. Mira also doesn't have much time, but she decides to spend just 10 minutes a day on building her skill. Let's say that Mira gets 1% better at archery each day she practices. If both Ada and Mira start off with a skill level of 1 (whatever that means), then after 365 days, Ada will be starting her "really do it" training at level 1, while Mira will already be at 1.01 ^ 365 = 37.8. That's a pretty stark difference.

Unfortunately, it works in both directions. If Mira instead adopted a negative habit that made her 1% worse at archery each day, 365 days would mean 0.99 ^ 365 = 0.025. We're still not sure what 37.8 or 0.025 mean in the context of archery, but the same concept applies to most skills. We've personally used the 10 minutes/day approach to learn Spanish and Italian, become fairly good at meditating, and even get pretty darn good at making cookies (or so we're told). You get the point—habits are powerful because of their cumulative effect. And of course, this effect isn't limited to skills. The effects of habits can determine our health, our relationships, and even the extent to which we're engaged with our lives.

> Try asking yourself—what is one thing that you can devote 10 minutes a day to getting better at? Ideally, something that doesn't require travel or significant investment. Try it out for 30 days (do 10 minutes of the thing each day) and see what happens. You might find that you're 1.347 times better than you were, but also you might find that you want to spend more than those 10 minutes doing it.

When performing their diary studies, Wood and her team wanted to understand what people were thinking about as they performed habitual actions. To what extent were they present and in control? Their results showed that, for the most part, individuals weren't mentally present as they repeated habits. Most people let their mind wander to anything other than what they were doing in the moment. Think about a route you've driven or walked a hundred times. For most of us, these trips happen almost unconsciously—unless, of course, you live in a city like Montreal (like your authors), where unexpected new potholes, construction, distracted drivers, and bicyclists keep any route from ever really becoming habitual.

This kind of automaticity is a commonly cited component of habits. In fact, automatic behavior is part of the definition of what makes a habit. In his work, (including a paper that has one of the best titles we've come across: *The Unbearable Automaticity of Being*), Yale psychologist John Bargh points out that habits tend to come with "the four horsemen of automaticity."[2] These four horsemen are efficiency, lack of awareness, unintentionality, and uncontrollability. Habits aren't just repetitive—they're unconscious.

Are Habits a Bad Thing?

Having a high percentage of fairly unconscious habitual states doesn't sound like the key to living an intentional life, but there's a wrinkle. While all habits are unintentional at the moment of execution, some are built on a strong foundation of intentions. If used correctly, habits are a tool to help us carry out our long-term goals. When we're able to build them with intention, habits are a superpower. But when formed unintentionally, they can be one of the most destructive forces in our lives as once they're set, they can have profound effects. Habits are a bit like a water slide—you can choose which tunnel to jump into (perhaps at random), but then it's pretty hard to change course.

The problem with habits, though, isn't that they're automatic. If anything, that's their strength. It's that habits are a long-term expression of a single moment in time, sustained by inner (e.g., feelings) and outer (e.g., objects) cues. They can be formed in moments of high intentionality, like when Sister Buder decided to put on that old pair of sneakers and start running ("training religiously"). But habits can also be formed in a moment of weakness, like when you felt stressed and decided to try that cigarette one day and were still smoking years later.

Habits as an Expression of Intentions

Habits are tools we can wield to carry out our intentions. In their 2014 study,[3] Marieke Adriaanse and her colleagues used empirical data to show something rather unintuitive. Historically, it's been assumed that higher baseline levels of self-control help people stay healthy by allowing them to resist temptation. If I'm able to resist that donut, it must be my uncanny ability to apply self-control at that instant and turn away from temptation. But as the team showed, despite how logical this assumption sounds, it is, in fact, untrue. Results from their study showed that the ability to apply self-control is more closely linked to the formation of adaptive habits. What does this mean? Healthy eaters, it turns out, don't have superhuman self-control in the moment; they're just good *habit-makers*. They're not necessarily better at resisting temptation; rather, they're better at building habits that avoid temptation in the first place. So even if willpower isn't your strength, not all hope is lost. Habits can be used to guide our intentions into reality, even more than sheer (and hopefully nonlimited) willpower.

Yet, most of us treat habits as fixed and willpower as a tool to compensate for them. We might think it's too late to cut out dessert every evening, but we convince ourselves we'll make it up by exercising the next morning. Unfortunately, this strategy rarely works, as you have probably experienced. Habits aren't a random series of actions thrust on us by the universe. They're the ghosts of our past goals (like going to bed early)—an imperative with no resistance that needs no current why.

The Natural Ease of Habits

Due to their automatic nature, habits tend to be easy to execute. But it isn't necessarily the nature of the action that's easy. Many habits are difficult or complex. The ease comes from following the path of least resistance. That's the power of habit loops.

The now-famous term *habit loop* was introduced by Charles Duhigg, a Pulitzer-prize winning journalist, in his book *The Power of Habit*,[4] and the term has since become widely used among psychiatrists, neuroscientists, and science communicators. The loop breaks habits down into three stages:

- ◆ **The Cue:** A trigger that sparks our need or desire to engage in a habit. These can be internal or external, like an alarm going off, a time of day, or a stressful feeling.
- ◆ **The Routine:** The habit, like your nightly bowl of ice cream, brushing your teeth, or checking your phone.
- ◆ **The Reward:** The result of the behavior, like the sweet taste of sugar, clean teeth, or the dopamine rush of social media.

Habit loops, along with associated concepts such as reinforcement, are some of the most studied concepts in neuroscience. Thanks to researchers like MIT's Dr. Ann Graybiel, we now know a lot about how the brain creates and maintains habits.[5] In her research in the late 1990s, Graybiel showed that activity in an area of the brain called the basal ganglia (in particular, the striatum) correlates with learning and execution of habitual actions.

The striatum is connected to many other parts of the brain and responsible for motor control and goal setting—it's also a big reason why habits feel so easy. Learning a habit requires considerable conscious attention and effort. But as the action starts to be repeated and tied to an expected reward, our brain rewires itself to make the action easier. Through something called Hebbian learning (as the old saying goes: "neurons that fire together wire together"), habits become more and more intertwined in the brain's dopaminergic system, requiring less cognitive effort with each repetition. Not only do our new habits get easier, but they also bring us a more significant reward. Our neurology, from this perspective, actively encourages the automation of habits.

As is often the case, however, the process of habit formation is more complex or nuanced than we might like. Because of the way habits are wired in our brains, they're often focused on obvious rewards, like a rush of glucose from eating candy or the false sense of being loved that "likes" on our feeds give us. So if our habit formation systems are left untamed, they remain biased toward short-term rewards over long-term rewards, which may run counter to the types of changes we are intentionally trying to make. The key to rewiring this system is through the reward stage.

For example, if our habit reward is too far away from our actions, it can be hard to establish a cycle. Taking a cold shower might feel great. . .but that feeling only comes 10 minutes after you've confronted the icy blast. Because there's a delay between the action and the reward, it takes an additional measure of conscious effort to rewire our brains to look forward to the boost we'll get later on. This is especially true during Montreal winters, when the substance coming out of the shower is closer to a frozen slush than a liquid. So perhaps you instead consciously tie the reward to the feeling of warmth you get when you jump out of the shower and into your waiting towel. In other words, as in all things, if we want effective habits, we have to apply our intention.

Building Intentional Habits

If you'd like to build a new habit from scratch, a good way to start is by being mindful of potential habit-building moments. As we learned, self-control is better applied in habit formation than resisting existing habits. Since habits tend to be cued by the environment around us, any kind of change in that environment can be an opportunity to build new habits. Just changed jobs? Pay attention to habits you form at your new workplace. Just moved to a new neighborhood? Be deliberate about how you spend your time as you settle in. Your new regular activity may become part of your life for years to come.

Similarly, we can adopt deliberate changes in our environment to create better habits. These changes also don't need to be as drastic as relocating your family. For example, if you'd like to read more, you can start by stopping by the library on your way home every Friday after work. Or if you'd like to be more physically active, you can rearrange your space at home to accommodate an exercise area.

Disrupting Negative Habits

Disrupting an existing habit is one of the more difficult challenges for our brain. As habits become ingrained, they become central parts of our identity—tackling them requires a slow and careful approach. One place to start is awareness. As research on addiction by Dr. Judson Brewer suggests,[6] awareness may represent somewhat of a brain hack in tackling habits. In the same way that our reward systems are such powerful drivers of maintaining habits, they can be used to subvert them. In Brewer and colleagues'[7] words: "Bringing awareness to one's subjective experience and behavior can produce a change in valuation of learned but unhealthy behaviors, leading to self-regulatory shifts that result in sustainable behavior change without force." Or more simply, once we are aware or mindful that we have gotten into a bad habit, that awareness alone may initiate a change in our behavior, thereby weakening the bad habit.

Applying awareness requires being mindful of loops that long ago became a habit. Start by identifying the behaviors that don't serve your goals, and begin to take note of potential triggers. Are you more likely to eat sweet or salty foods when you're stressed? Do you check your phone every time you get a notification? Once you're aware of your habit loop, think deeply about the reward you get from it. Is it all that it's cracked up to be? Is it possible that a more meaningful reward that aligns with your values and intention is available somewhere else? Do you think that people who eat healthy food generally feel better or worse? By remembering to ask ourselves these kinds of questions and feeling what the results of our actions are, Brewer contends, we can successfully rewire habit loops.

Once you've increased awareness of your habits, you can begin to rewire your brain. While it might seem like a daunting task, you don't need a neuroscience degree to start manipulating your own reward systems. You can start by understanding the values-rich habit cycle, created by clinical psychologist Diana Hill.[8] This approach provides alternative habits to target the emotions that your current habits fulfill.[9] By rerouting these benefits through habits that align with your values, you can disrupt and rebuild habit loops. Of course, this is easier said than done. We explore how to disrupt and rebuild habits in the next chapter, but as a start, let's think a bit more about the components of some of your habits.

To do this, try this circle of control exercise:

1. To start, write down a habit that you would like to change or disrupt—as a generic but important example, let's take eating healthier.
2. Now, take a piece of paper and draw three circles, each within the other (like a dart board).
3. In the center circle, write down everything related to that habit that you have complete control over—for example, writing down a grocery list and then sticking to it at the store, learning a new recipe, or avoiding eating at fast food restaurants.
4. In the middle circle, write down things related to eating that you cannot control but can still influence in some way—for example, how hungry you feel, how you feel about salads, how much stress you experience at work, and so on.
5. In the outermost circle, write down aspects of your life related to eating that affect you but over which you don't feel you have any control or influence—for example, the food habits you were brought up with or the price of healthy food items.

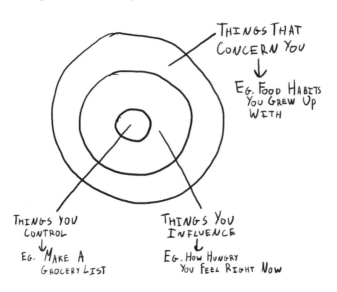

THINGS THAT
CONCERN YOU
↓
EG. FOOD HABITS
YOU GREW UP
WITH

THINGS YOU
CONTROL
EG. MAKE A
GROCERY LIST

THINGS YOU
INFLUENCE
EG. HOW HUNGRY
YOU FEEL RIGHT NOW

Take a look at your circles. Are you applying emotional and physical energy on the right parts of the circle? In theory you should be using tools in the center circle to affect things in the middle one, and should be spending very little emotional energy on those in the outer circles. Obviously, this is easier said than done—you need to find solutions that work for you, your habits, and your life. Not everyone can go on a quick jog after work instead of taking a smoke break. If you're at a loss for structuring your day to avoid negative habits, try incorporating a leading habit creation strategy: stacking.

Stacking Your Habits

Think of your habits as a piece of computer code, automatically executed at regular time intervals. While it may be difficult to change the code, adding a small snippet to it is a bit easier. This is called habit stacking—using existing habits as an anchor for new ones.

Habit stacking is a form of implementation intention, a premeditated plan about your future actions. It was popularized by James Clear, the author of *Atomic Habits* whom is referred to in Chapter 25. His formula is simple:[10]

After/Before [CURRENT HABIT], I will [NEW HABIT].

This method makes use of the fact that half our lives are habits. Instead of saying you'll start stretching every day—and pushing it off—tie it to a different daily habit. After you complete your nightly routine of brushing your teeth and washing your face, stretch for 10 minutes before you get into bed. Once you have your stretching routine down pat, you can add something else. After you brush your teeth, wash your face, and stretch, list three things you're grateful for before getting into bed. By habit stacking, you can create your own, intentional cues for habits—rinsing your face is the cue for getting out your yoga mat; rolling up your mat is your cue to start your gratitude list.

Rewire Your Own Brain

Our brains are built to identify goals, prioritize them, and turn the most rewarding ones into habits. This reduces the amount of goal-directed thinking we have to apply and frees us up to think about other goals. Our brains are trying to do us a favor with this setup—unfortunately, the most immediately rewarding goals aren't necessarily the ones we want. An intentional approach to habits means being a more active participant in the process of creation.

Let's recap our takeaways:

- Be more cognizant when your brain is creating a new habit, and force yourself to ask: "Is this really something I'd like to start doing unconsciously all the time?"
- Build on the fact that habits are cued by the environment to use changes in your environment as tools to change habits.
- Create a deeper awareness of the rewards associated with existing habits.
- Habit-stack around existing habits as a way to more quickly adopt new ones.

With nearly half of our lives made up of habits, learning how to form new ones and disrupt unwanted ones can take us a long way toward a more intentional life. The process may be hard, but failing to set intentional habits is like failing to set up an autopilot to the right destination—the eventual results will not be welcome. As you think about what you'd like your habits to look like, know that this is a challenge for all of us (including the three authors of this book). Challenging ourselves to go for what we want, however, can be hugely rewarding.

CHAPTER 27

Finding the Power Within

"No man is free who is not master of himself."

—Epictetus

When Dan was 16 years old, he fell in love with Federico Fellini's *8½*. Each time Marcello Mastroianni appeared onscreen, Dan was struck by his effortless charm. Something about the quiet power with which he dominated the screen. He had never been to Italy, but the more he engaged with its culture, the more he knew that's where he belonged.

On one trip to Italy, he made a list of restaurants in Rome, hidden gems other tourists didn't know about. Another time, he visited a micro-producer in the north and learned that high quality fresh olive oil—the real stuff—has a hint of pepper and is almost bitter. With each trip, he realized Italy was his calling. If only he spoke the language.

But how hard could it be? He set aside time each day for learning vocab and grammar. He bought a language-learning program and followed it religiously. In the beginning, everything went smoothly. It felt as effortless as Mastroianni's character looked on screen. But soon, he would open his Italian grammar book and feel a twang of dread. Visions of speaking with Nonnas in the Sicilian countryside were replaced with mild anxiety about studying. Learning Italian became a chore.

What happened? How could a habit meant to facilitate his passion feel so painful? He wasn't lazy. He didn't lose his attentional focus. He certainly didn't lose his love of all things Italian. The answer was one of motivation. In fact, Dan's lack of enthusiasm can be explained by a groundbreaking motivational theory from one of psychology's biggest rebels.

The Behavioral Zeitgeist of the 1970s

The 1970s had no shortage of rebels. From Andy Warhol and Joan Jett to Hunter S. Thompson and Gloria Steinem, breaking down barriers was the path to becoming a cultural icon. One iconoclast you might not know well is Edward Deci: the rebel behaviorist.

Behaviorism is the school of thought, advanced in the early 20th century, which proposes that our behaviors are brought on by conditioning from the outside world. You are no doubt familiar with behaviorism even if you've never heard of it by name. World-famous researchers like John Watson, B.F. Skinner, and Ivan Pavlov (as well as his dogs) all contributed to the field, paving the way for some of the most influential and fundamental concepts in psychology. These concepts haven't just helped us understand how our minds work, but have also contributed to our ability to build artificial minds by copying some of those mechanisms (e.g., with reinforcement learning).

However, as much as behaviorism was helpful in advancing psychology and neuroscience, the concepts of behaviorism seemed to lack some humanity. Then along came Deci.

Deci was an experimental psychology professor at the University of Rochester. Though trained in behaviorism, Deci was inclined to think of human action as more than just a sum of environmental cues. He felt strongly that humans are proactive and engaged players in their own life—Main Characters, if you will. He suggested an extension to behaviorism that would make room for our sense of agency.

Deci began the first steps toward self-determination theory with his 1971 SOMA cube experiment. He gave two groups of participants a mathematical puzzle to solve: a 3D cube that could be dissected and reassembled. One group was paid to solve the cube, while the other group was unpaid. After the task, Deci would tell the puzzle-solver that he needed to step out for a few minutes, and they could entertain themselves in the meantime. Those who were paid to solve the cube chose to peruse the nearby magazines. But those who weren't paid? They went back to playing with the cube.

Deci's SOMA cube experiment was one of the first to show that rewards can actually *disincentivize behavior* (contrary to what behaviorism would predict). But despite his findings—or perhaps because of them—Deci remained an outcast in the scientific community. He had made many enemies in the behavioralist community due to his views, and his experiment only made it worse. It was during this time that Deci ran into Richard Ryan on the University of Rochester campus. Ryan had a philosophical background, and he too was interested in challenging the status quo.

Together, they embarked on an experimental program resulting in their 1985 book *Intrinsic Motivation and Self-Determination in Human Behavior* (which is mentioned briefly in Chapter 9). Self-determination theory, one of the most influential modern motivation models, was born.

What Drives Us When No One Is Looking?

Self-determination theory (SDT) suggests there are three basic human needs that motivate self-initiated behaviors: autonomy, competence, and relatedness. Competence means we want to improve at the tasks we choose; relatedness means we want to connect with others. But for our purposes when discussing intention and awareness, we want to focus on autonomy.

Deci and Ryan found that offering external incentives to encourage certain behaviors could wind up disincentivizing those same behaviors. A great example of this is the incentive to donate blood. According to World Health Organization reports, countries that only engage with voluntary blood donation consistently have more donors than countries with paid blood donation.[1]

What do we get out of voluntary blood donations? The most successful predictor of donations isn't money, or free snacks, but altruism.[2] We donate blood out of the kindness of our hearts (and all the extra blood we have pumping around in there). If we're given money for our blood, this removes the intrinsic incentive. Sure, we can say we're donating blood for the good of others, but at the end of the day, we're being paid for our services. Eventually, our motivation will transition from intrinsic to extrinsic—from altruism to a financial incentive—which isn't as effective. Why? Because it undermines our need for autonomy.

None of this should be particularly surprising—self-determination theory has made its way to the mainstream and has been the dominant way of thinking about motivation for decades. But how does self-determination theory help explain the invisible wall we hit on the third week of a new habit? If the habit we've created is aligned with our deep long-term goal of living in Italy, then why is it that we seem to block it each time we sit down to study? The answer lies in something called *identified regulation*.

The Beginner's Guide to Extrinsic Motivation

One of the core tenets of self-determination theory is that motivation exists on a continuum, which looks roughly like this:

On the left side, we have amotivation, an automatic state of unconsciously not caring about the thing. Then, toward the right, we move into the realm of extrinsic motivation—tasks are motivating, but for external rewards. Finally, on the far right hand side, we reach intrinsic motivation, where tasks are motivating for their own sake. Let's see what these look like from the point of view of learning a language:

- ◆ **Amotivation:** You have no motivation to learn Italian. You don't see the point in it, you don't enjoy it, and you don't think it will lead to any useful outcomes. Think of someone who feels forced to study a language in school, but doesn't see any personal benefit, and thus, puts in minimal effort.
- ◆ **Extrinsic Motivation:**
  - • **External Regulation:** You're learning Italian because of an external reward or punishment, like passing a class, or because your parents will reward you for good grades (perhaps even a trip to Italy!).
  - • **Introjected Regulation:** You're learning Italian because you feel an internal pressure or obligation, like a feeling of guilt for not knowing it. After all, you *are* of Italian heritage.
  - • **Identified Regulation:** You're learning Italian because you recognize and agree with the importance of the task. In this case, knowing Italian will be beneficial for your career or travel ambitions. Boxes checked.
  - • **Integrated Regulation:** You're learning Italian because it aligns with your broader goals and values, even though the activity itself may not be inherently enjoyable. Maybe you value multicultural understanding and see language learning as part of your identity. No pain, no gain.
- ◆ **Intrinsic Motivation:** You're learning Italian because you find the process itself enjoyable and satisfying. You love the way the words sound, you enjoy the challenge of mastering the grammar, and you get a kick out of being able to read Italian literature.

While learning Italian to integrate into the culture may, at first glance, seem like an intrinsically motivated habit, it's actually somewhere between identified regulation and integrated regulation. As much as learning Italian is aligned with Dan's values and goals, he's doing it in order to achieve something—whether to make traveling in Italy easier or because he feels like speaking Italian is an identity he aspires to have, learning Italian remains just a means to an end (telic as opposed to atelic activity, as is discussed in Chapter 11).

And perhaps this is completely fine when the learning is easy, as Dan has less friction to overcome, and therefore, needs less motivation. However, as he advances and the learning gets harder, friction increases, and the extrinsic motivation may no longer be enough to overcome it. This is likely the wall that he's hitting. In fact, this is the wall we all hit when we apply self-discipline toward a long-term goal. Discipline can feel painful and unsettling when an activity aligned with our aspirations begins to feel agency-robbing. So, how do we resolve this internal conflict? How do we get ourselves into the feels-good intrinsic motivation column?

Hijacking the Brain's Reward Systems with Awareness

The fact that such a large part of our aspirations and goals is based on relatively weak extrinsic motivators might feel a bit demoralizing. However, this kind of assessment, which many of us apply to our lives and use as a rationale to stop advancing, isn't all that accurate. As we'll see, the problem isn't that these activities aren't intrinsically motivating; we just haven't properly integrated them into our reward circuits.

Dr. Judson Brewer, who is discussed in Chapters 8 and 26, is an American psychiatrist who has dedicated his career to studying the neuroscience of negative behavior patterns, from stress eating and smoking, to anxiety and anger. With his colleagues, Brewer has shown that effective behavior change comes not from forcing ourselves but through something called autonomous self-regulation—which means that the behavior change is self-initiated.[3]

The key to their work is acknowledging that humans are reward-driven. Of course, we want to take an easy drive instead of sweating on our bike. Of course, we want to watch a streaming series instead of hitting the Italian grammar books. Our brains love easy rewards. However, increased mindfulness can help us rewire undesirable behaviors and find lasting appreciation for our target behaviors. We may even come to understand that effective self-discipline is not found in forcing ourselves to do something we don't like but in finding how we can genuinely appreciate the behavior we would like to make into a habit.

61% of people believe that discipline is about forcing themselves to do things they don't enjoy.

It might sound like a far-fetched idea that mindfulness would lead the way to solving our motivation dilemma, but Brewer's clinical results have surpassed any and all expectations. When we're aware of the effects of our behaviors, we can better understand how our actions impact our well-being. The key, of course, is to make the conscious link in a way that motivates us to take our desired action. Research has proven that autonomously driven behavior change is far more successful than controlled behavior change,[4] spanning habits like weight loss, smoking, and exercise.

But the abstract idea of "being mindful" can be hard to translate into actionable strategies. Fortunately for us, Brewer and his colleagues have identified seven easy points in the habit loop which, in combination, can help us rewire our reward systems. This means that when we commit to increasing our awareness at these key moments, we can move more easily from forcing ourselves to keep up our habits (which means they're likely not truly habits but repeated actions), to an unforced, self-initiated effort (and true habit). Set out in the following section are the seven steps to doing this, and we would encourage you to think of a habit that you'd like to change as you read through them.

The Seven Steps to Rewire Our Habits

STEP 1: BE AWARE OF GOAL-INCONGRUENT BEHAVIOR (BEHAVIORS THAT DON'T LINE UP WITH OUR GOALS)

The first step is to choose a habit and concretize it as much as possible. Think about a habit you'd like to change—it could be something negative you'd like to eliminate (excessive screen time, unhealthy eating and smoking are common ones) or something positive you'd like to reinforce (drinking more water, reading more, and meditating are ones that our research has found to be popular).

Picture yourself performing the habit. What exactly are you doing? Imagine each tiny action in detail—picture the smells, the noises around you, the way your body feels.

First, examine all of the behaviors that support this habit. Given that this is a habit you'd like to change, chances are it's supported by behaviors you'd also like to change. For example, if your target habit is to reduce screen time, perhaps you realize that scrolling through social media while lying in bed isn't in line with your long-term goals. This first step isn't about deep or complex analysis of the unwanted behaviors. All it takes is noting that the behaviors that aren't aligned with our goals exist.

STEP 2: BE AWARE OF THE RESULTS OF GOAL-INCONGRUENT BEHAVIOR

The second step is about becoming aware of the effects of these behaviors. In practice, this could look like paying attention to how you feel before, during, and after the behavior in question. A common question that follows this stage is: "what if the behavior still feels good?" This step can be a helpful tool for differentiating between enjoyment and over-indulgence. Watching an episode of a popular new series isn't a bad behavior. But binge-watching so many episodes that you're not getting enough sleep will likely have adverse effects on our well-being. By practicing awareness in the present moment, we can evaluate whether certain behaviors are hurting our long-term goals or not.

In their study, Brewer and colleagues propose that linking action to outcome can help update the reward centers in the brain. If we start to associate eating a bag of potato chips with the bloated feeling we experience afterward, instead of the initial salty satisfaction, we may be able to rewire our cravings.

STEP 3: BE AWARE OF THE TRIGGERS OF GOAL-INCONGRUENT BEHAVIOR (RECOGNIZE WHAT SEEMS TO INITIATE A BEHAVIOR THAT DOESN'T SUPPORT OUR GOAL)

Though many of us may be aware of our triggers, they're often easier to identify after understanding the habit loop formation. This step in behavior change requires paying attention to the inciting or initiating instances that lead us to engage in certain behaviors—these can range from feeling stressed to the smell of a bakery in the morning. This step asks us to be attuned to the situations and feelings that trigger our unwanted behaviors.

STEP 4: BE AWARE OF FORCED OR EFFORTFUL RESTRAINT OF BEHAVIOR

What do we do when faced with a trigger or craving? Often, we try to fight it. As we arrive home from work, stressed and hungry, we ignore the bag of potato chips sitting in our cupboard. We simply push down the urge to start munching on chips. We engage in robot mode.

As another simple step of awareness, this point asks individuals to become aware of the feelings they experience when they try to resist a tempting behavior. Paying more attention can make us aware of how draining and unpleasant these feelings are. Robot mode can make us feel unmotivated or lower our mood—we're stressed, overworked, and now we can't even enjoy our favorite snack? The key here is that by allowing ourselves to feel what we are feeling we can start to become aware of the effects of those feelings.

STEP 5: BE AWARE OF THE RESULTS OF FORCE OR EFFORTFUL RESTRAINT OF BEHAVIOR

While resisting our cravings, like enjoying the salty taste of the chips, can lead to positive outcomes, such forceful resisting comes with negative feelings, too. In fact, these strained responses can result in poor psychological health, emotional breakdowns.[5,6] The effort it takes to resist temptations can be draining—and this is why robot mode isn't a sustainable solution for many/most people.

Although robot mode may be what most folks reach for first, we believe that unforced effort will actually be more effective. The first step is simple awareness. Don't fight the craving; pay attention to it. By paying attention to feelings we have been trying to resist, we might notice how soon the craving re-emerges. Do we crave potato chips every time we have a busy day at work? The short-term goal is to better understand the draining nature of robot mode. The long-term goal is to understand that white-knuckled willpower isn't a sustainable strategy. Once we're aware of the impact this take-no-prisoners strategy has on us, we're less likely to choose it in the future. Instead, we can start to shift to unforced effort.

STEP 6: BE AWARE OF CHOICE AND EXPLORE NEW, AUTONOMOUSLY MOTIVATED BEHAVIORS

Once we're aware of what partaking in goal-incongruent behaviors feels like, and what it's like to try and avoid tempting choices, we can start to explore the third option: autonomously motivated behaviors.

With our heightened awareness, we know eating the potato chips makes us feel bloated and oversaturated with sodium. We also know that resisting the temptation of the chips feels frustrating and draining. Where do we go from here? We address our behavior at the root—our desire for potato chips.

In fact, one of Brewer's clients had a habit of eating a bag of potato chips each night. She couldn't stop—the salty crunch was too hard to eliminate from her life. But once she began practicing mindfulness around her eating habits, she was able to find her natural limits. When she really paid attention to the taste and feeling of the potato chips, over time, she found her limit was exactly two potato chips. Any more, and she'd start to feel the sodium overdose making its way through her taste buds. She found that eating two potato chips was more satisfying than making her way through the bag and feeling bloated—which was a realization that she could not have forced herself into.

Other examples of exploration might look like fitting your morning stretching routine into your evening plans instead. Maybe it involves switching from karate to dance classes, or going for a brisk walk when you feel stressed instead of trying to meditate.

STEP 7: BE AWARE OF THE RESULTS OF NEW, AUTONOMOUS BEHAVIORS

Once you start exploring, you can start to pay attention to how different behaviors make you feel, physically, mentally, and emotionally. Ms. Two-Potato-Chips, as Brewer likes to refer to his previous patient, felt a physical improvement from her behavior change—and she still got to taste her favorite snack each day.

Perhaps stretching out at night, while requiring some schedule shifting, makes you feel well-rested before bed, instead of the fatigue you feel when trying to do it at 6 a.m. Maybe replacing your weekend karate with dance classes makes you excited for cardio, and for the musical and social aspect that comes with it. When we're in a mindful state every day, we rely less on traditional self-regulatory strategies like avoidance, distraction, and suppression.[7] Practicing awareness can kick our need to engage in robot mode.

Paying attention to the effects of our behaviors—both desirable and undesirable—means we can rewire our reward systems to favor what our minds and bodies really need. Slowing down to mindfully pay attention to what feels good allows us to make clearer decisions about which behaviors to partake in, which increases our enthusiasm. We can intentionally align our values and our actions in ways that increase our sense of being rewarded. We really can have our cake and eat it, too—just like Dan, who is now pretty proficient in Italian—ciao, Dan!

CHAPTER 28

The Importance of Workplace Rituals

"In the midst of an assembly that is full of life and activity, sensations are felt, and emotions are awakened in the individual that are unknown in private life. These new impressions come to him not only from the very fact of the gathering, but also from the special practices that are followed on these occasions."

—Emile Durkheim

At Stickyeyes, a U.K.-based marketing agency, the completion of every successful project is marked by the project lead hitting a gong. With a Nerf gun. Their head of Design & Development, Andy Duke, explains the intention behind the ritual: "We found a common problem within design teams is the temptation to jump straight into the next project as soon as one ends. We wanted to create a culture that encouraged designers to take time, reflect, and enjoy the successful end of a project."[1]

Hitting the gong is not exactly a habit at Stickyeyes. It's a ritual. What's the difference? While both are done "habitually," they're actually quite different. Habits tend to have a *raison-d'être* that is derived from the action itself. We brush our teeth to have good dental hygiene. We do a crossword puzzle each week to keep our mind sharp. A ritual is different—a ritual transcends the end result and holds an underlying meaning. When I hit a gong with a Nerf gun, I'm not just shooting the gong for the sake of it or to improve my aim. I'm celebrating a job well done.

Due to their respective natures, habits tend to be individual, while rituals generally tend to be collective. But there can also be collective habits. Raffaela Giovagnoli, a philosophy professor at the Pontifical Lateran University in Vatican City, distinguishes between I-mode habits and We-mode habits.[2] I-mode habits include the classics like brushing our teeth. We-mode habits might look like grabbing drinks with a sibling every Thursday or going to a regular religious service with your family on a weekend morning.

Because human rituals are symbolic, they're more than just We-habits. When we cross a stage in a cap and gown to receive a diploma, the rolled paper is not what provides us value. Nor is it the silly-looking hat that makes our loved ones clap or shed a tear. Rituals come in many forms, but each represents a larger idea—it's the shared context that provides the meaning. And that meaning has a very real effect on us, either personally or as a group.

Rituals are there in part to decrease anxiety and improve our performance in everything from public speaking to first dates.[3] How does that work? Participating in rituals affects us in three core ways:[4]

- First, they help us regulate our emotions. When we perform rituals after a loss—for example, hosting a funeral or wake after losing a loved one—rituals help alleviate our grief.[5]
- Second, rituals can also help us achieve certain psychological states, like athletes who prepare for a competition with a set of repeated actions, or students who perform an action for luck before a test.
- Third, performing rituals also helps us feel connected with others. By partaking in a game-day ritual with friends, we emphasize and reinforce our shared bond over our team. Even when rituals are done when we're all alone, they are often an attempt to connect with a broader community—often our families or other folks who have faith in the power of that ritual. And believe it or not, rituals change our brains.

The Power of Workplace Rituals

But how much do they change our brains? "It's not that we do rituals and then, magically, we like doing our work later that day," Harvard behavioral scientist Michael Norton explains. "It's that over time, rituals themselves become meaningful to us—a sense of 'this is how we do things around here.'"[6] Rituals can give us a sense of accomplishment, camaraderie, or belief in ourselves. That's a game changer.

Too many leaders focus on managing teams as a set of individuals, rather than being intentional about the interactions among team members. In this context, workplace rituals are a useful way to create meaningful work experience for employees and improve team alignment on common goals and team members' relationships.[7] By intentionally building a set of well-thought-out rituals—and remembering to adapt them as time goes on—leaders and team members can dramatically improve workplace harmony and the sense of shared intention in their teams.

Just like individual habits, workplace rituals support our intention by reinforcing a team's focus on the behaviors needed to achieve their goals—think of Stickeyes' desire to reinforce celebration of a job well done. But they have a secondary benefit as well: reinforcing a sense of connection and togetherness. As Tami Kim explained to us in our conversation with her: "Upon completing a group ritual, people are much more likely to imbue the subsequent task with more meaning, which, in turn, leads to better work performance. If you think about rituals that exist in the world—walking a specific route before a sports game, ringing a gong after a successful deal, taping the first dollar earned to the wall—they inherently don't really serve a direct instrumental purpose. But the specific characteristics of group rituals—physical movements, symbolism, communality— help amplify the meaning inherent in a ritual, which can then spill over to subsequent tasks that individuals must complete."[8]

The Need for Workplace Rituals

Workplace rituals can be divided into two categories, though many activities can overlap. The first category consists of habits that are fundamental to productivity. This can include morning check-ins or using certain communication technologies at specific times. The second category encompasses rituals that are focused on building team cohesion, like Friday afternoon happy hours. Despite the fact that productivity rituals are taken more seriously, and team-building rituals are seen as a nice-to-have, we have seen both kinds of rituals be instrumental in fostering intentional teams.

> 73% of people think workplace rituals are useful.

During the COVID-induced debates on working from home (WFH), the conversation shifted focus from productivity to culture. Initially, many opponents to WFH policies doubted that teams would be as productive. But studies have shown that productivity actually increases in some remote working environments (at least for simple individual tasks like call center work—a 2014 study of Chinese workers found that working from home led to a 13% performance increase, due to more time, fewer sick days, and a quieter and more convenient working environment).[9] As more research comes in, this may shift, but the important point for us is that this is only half the equation of what's important in a workplace.

Rituals come into play when the conversation focuses on a different challenge: the need to somehow create cohesive cultures for remote and hybrid workforces. While working remotely has a variety of benefits, it's unable to facilitate the type of culture that comes naturally to in-person workplaces. The answer lies in creating and sustaining successful workplace rituals—recall their third benefit: building social bonds with others.

As Nicholas Bloom told us in a recent discussion, due to the massive issues around creating cohesive cultures with fully remote workforces, only about 13% of workers are fully remote, and these tend to be contractual workers (call centers, IT support, payments processing, etc.) where the need to have a sense of belonging and an understanding of the shared intentions of the company are much lower.[10] For more crucial roles, regardless of the structure of remote, hybrid, or in-person work, rituals are an important ingredient in creating a set of shared intentions in those teams.

The Benefits of Workplace Rituals

By ritualizing productive habits, teams can ensure these best practices are used as effectively as possible. In order to take these practices from chore to ritual, the practice must always be in service to a greater goal—and should never create extra work for the team. Morning or daily check-ins are a perfect example: A quick conversation with all team members present offers the opportunity to share progress, discuss impediments, and solicit help. Each check-in helps create accountability among team members. Together, the check-ins facilitate communication and build alignment on shared objectives.

But the most important effect of check-ins is the one it has on the softer side of the equation. In fact, rituals like check-ins are the most effective form of establishing a sense of belonging for employees. Across all ages and genders, nearly 40% of workers feel the greatest sense of belonging when colleagues check in with them—both personally and professionally.[11] Just because a workplace habit is implemented to increase productivity, doesn't mean it can't fulfill a cultural purpose as well. These shared social experiences are what bind teams together. Whether this is on the margins of the ritual (like a social catch-up before the start of the official morning check-in) or the focus (like a happy hour), opportunities to build community outside of individual tasks is invaluable.

What is interesting is that in order to be effective and considered valuable to workers and management, *the more focused these activities are on shared intentions the better.* As one study found, the two types of team-building activities that respondents found to be most valuable and most effective were volunteer days (where participants collectively support a charitable cause) and company retreats (where things like company strategy and direction are discussed).[12]

The best workplace rituals are ones that build the team and its individuals at the same time—and reinforce desired behaviors. For example, a quarterly awards program that celebrates team members' achievements, from sales to mentoring to creativity, serves multiple goals. The awards program reinforces the team's values by celebrating what is important to them, motivates competitive team members, and recognizes those who work the hardest.

That said, let's remember to celebrate the right behaviors by designing rituals that align with our intentions. As an example, when he was a consultant, Mike once had a client who wanted her organization to be more innovative—so she put in place an annual award for innovation, hoping to motivate her team to become more creative. The problem? At the inaugural ceremony, she wanted to celebrate an employee who came up with a product that, in its first year alone, had already generated over $100,000 of profit. Although that employee sounded like a good candidate at first glance, further consideration revealed that the award would be celebrating profit creation, not innovation. Instead, she found another employee who had piloted a failed offering, ultimately costing the company $20,000. The recipient was asked to prepare an acceptance speech that highlighted what they had learned in the process. By celebrating the learning that came with experimentation (as opposed to just celebrating a win), the organization signaled that trying new approaches was what they were after, and by making the award an annual event, the company was building a ritual that would bring a myriad of other benefits.

Choosing Workplace Rituals

The rituals you choose are important—simple rituals (like cheering together or firing a Nerf toy gun to conclude a project) can lead to a 16% increase in how meaningful employees judge their work to be.[13] The problem is that there's no one ritual that will create the perfect company culture. As with personal habits, workplace rituals should be continuously adapted to ensure they are updated alongside team goals. If left unchecked for too long, they can start to become constraints themselves. Even the most effective rituals can get stale if participants no longer believe in their objectives and simply comply out of requirement. For example, morning check-ins are no longer effective when participants aren't engaged with their team members, or preparing for a check-in becomes burdensome or performative.

The bottom line is that the most important thing is to imbue rituals with meaning, which shouldn't be a surprise to you after all of our talk about values and intention. This meaning can come from repetition over time, but it can also be accelerated by ensuring that the participants see the rituals as something unique to the team and important. Keeping our rituals fresh and meaningful drives our sense of engagement, resulting in greater feelings of belonging as well as greater productivity.

PART VII

Closing

CHAPTER 29

Intention in Our Relationships

"The clearest message that we get from our 75-year study is this: Good relationships keep us happier and healthier. Period."

—Robert Waldinger, director of the
Harvard Study of Adult Development[1]

For many of us, relationships are the most important aspect of our lives and as such, an important place for us to be intentional. Science backs this up: in a meta-analysis that looked at nearly 150 studies covering more than 300,000 participants, it was found that individuals with stronger social relationships had a whopping 50% higher likelihood of long-term survival compared to those with insufficient relationships.[2] Strong relationships don't just make us happier, they have a significant effect on our immune systems,[3] mental health,[4] and whether we develop dementia.[5]

Although this is all well known, what's less known is that relationships can even change how we experience pain. Dr. Naomi Eisenberger is a social psychologist at University of California, Los Angeles who studies the neural basis of social connection. In a 2011 study, Eisenberger and her colleagues investigated how attachment figures (people we feel close to) affect our perception of pain.[6] They asked female participants who were in long-term relationships to go through a physically painful experience (in this case, burning heat) while looking at photos of their loved one. The control group looked at photos of strangers or random objects. They found that those who looked at photos of their loved ones reported feeling less pain than those who looked at meaningless images.

Since brain activity was tracked in an fMRI scanner, researchers were able to see exactly how the human brain reacted in each circumstance. When the women looked at their loved ones, the areas of the brain that experience pain were less activated. Eisenberger and her colleagues hypothesized that attachment figures provide us with a sense of safety and security, which changes our neurochemical response to pain. In this way, our close relationships can act as a protection mechanism against painful experiences—both emotional and physical.

It shouldn't surprise us that relationships are central to our well-being. Whether from romantic relationships, family, or friends, regular interactions with people who know and love us are crucial and an obvious place for us to use our intentionality to help achieve our goals. As Robert Waldinger, the director of Harvard's study of human development, explains: the healthiest 80-year-olds are those who were the most satisfied with their relationships at 50 years old.[7]

What Makes a Family?

For many of us, the most central relationships that we have are those with our families. But the nature of what constitutes a family has changed dramatically over time. In the middle of the 19th century in the United States, nearly 70% of senior citizens lived with their children, but by the end of the 20th century, that number fell below 15%.[8] Fast-forward to the 21st century and now, for the first time since the Great Depression, more young adults are living with their parents than in any other living arrangement.[9] There's even been an increase in platonic co-parenting, a family structure in which two or more friends raise a child, instead of doing so in a traditionally romantic relationship.[10] The nature of families is fluid and ever-changing.

As our society continues to open up to different configurations of "family," we see the increased popularity of the idea of *chosen families*: those created by their members intentionally, instead of due to birth or marriage. Websites offer opportunities to share houses and parenting duties with strangers, harking back to multigenerational households. As the traditional construct of family continues to expand, the need to be intentional about our families—how we think about them, how we construct them, and how we interact with them—becomes even more important.

When we intentionally consider someone as a member of our family, we are acknowledging the quality and significance of the bond we share. This means that we are intentionally committed to each other and share a sense of responsibility for each other's well-being—whether our bond is by blood or by choice. From a psychological standpoint, being a family member may be the hardest job many of us will have. Families test our ability to stay present, regulate our emotions, and sacrifice our own interests. Because we can't easily walk away from our families, there is a deeper level of work required to be an intentional member of a family, whatever our role in the family may be. Of course, families are also a great source of deep connection, belonging, and good times, which makes the work to stay connected worth it. And all of the aspects of intention we've discussed in the preceding chapters come into play here—willpower, curiosity, integrity, attention, and habits (especially rituals!). But within relationships, we also have another level of responsibility in terms of helping others to be more intentional themselves.

Bringing Intention into Our Relationships

As leaders, educators, friends, or parents, our journey includes the role of being intentional role models for those around us. While our own personal benefits may be what sustain our drive for living with intention, inspiring others to live more intentionally will likely have ongoing effects that outweigh and outlast the benefits we experience ourselves. This form of paying it forward has tremendous positive impact—especially when we consider the exponential nature of our potential influence.

Other People Have Intention, Too?

In early chapters, we have discussed how shared intentionality is one of our superpowers as a species. Shared intentionality allows us to take ideas from one person's head, share them with others, and build systems that collectively move us toward those ideas. One of the key features of our psychology that allows us to do this is the Theory of Mind—our ability to surmise what's happening in the minds of others.

A classic test of the Theory of Mind is the Sally-Anne Test. Children are shown two dolls, named Sally and Anne. Sally has a basket and Anne has a box. In the course of the test, the child participants are shown Sally placing a marble in her basket. Then the Sally doll "leaves the room" and the sneaky Anne doll steals the marble and places it in her box instead. When Sally "returns," the child is asked where Sally will look for her marble. Children too young to understand the Theory of Mind will say the box—they know that's where the marble is. They don't understand that the Sally doll doesn't know the marble is there. But as they age, children will indicate the original basket, demonstrating their ability to understand the differing minds of others. They're able to look at the world through Sally's eyes.

Helping Others Be More Intentional

Whether in families or in groups outside of our families, we can help others to be more intentional, but that requires that we see the world from their point of view just like the children looking at the world through Sally's eyes. It also requires that we play the long game by helping to instill an attitude and long-term perspective regarding intentionality that goes beyond the current instance or project. That is, we focus on their learning how to be intentional, rather than simply solving the immediate problem or making the right intentional decision in the moment. We see four main steps to doing this well—starting with independence, giving freedom but not license, giving a helpful push, and supporting long-term thinking.

STEP 1: START WITH INDEPENDENCE

Making decisions for ourselves is a skill humans need to practice from early on—we can't live intentionally without it. For parents, part of helping a child learn to live intentionally is helping the child navigate an educational system designed to increase conformity. While there's real value in learning how to conform to societal expectations, ensuring that kids stay creative and independent wherever possible is important for the strengthening of their agency and their intentionality. As Picasso said, "Every child is an artist. The problem is how to remain an artist once we grow up." In order to remain artists, we believe that our children must cultivate intention.

As humans, our brains aren't fully developed until we're in our mid to late 20s.[11] And in our first few years of life, we require full-time support. Consequently, parents can get attached to the idea that they need to make all the choices for their kids as they grow. But as soon as possible, children should be given the chance to make their own, real choices. Even toddlers are capable of picking between foods to eat or stating a preference about which clothing to wear. By seeing the world through the child's eyes, we can realize the more we decide things for them, the more we limit their ability to decide for themselves.

In a work context, leaders should also question themselves on why they think they must tell their colleagues exactly what to do all the time. One of the greatest challenges, especially for new leaders in a corporate environment, is giving more independence to the people that work with and for us.

STEP 2: GIVE FREEDOM, NOT LICENSE

Freedom and responsibility are inherently connected. The consequences of our choices must inform the choices we make. And so, children need both freedom and responsibility. "Freedom, not license" is the motto of the Summerhill School, a private boarding school in England where children choose their own curriculum and are given the space to self-govern. A. S. Neill, the original founder of Summerhill, based his educational philosophy on schools fitting the child, rather than the reverse. As he explained, children are far more capable than we've come to believe: "A child is innately wise and realistic. If left to himself without adult suggestion of any kind, he will develop as far as he is capable of developing."[12] His book *Summerhill* led to the free school movement worldwide in the 1960s and 1970s, which remains a popular alternative to traditional education to this day.

The way that free schools recognize the importance of giving children freedom and responsibility is by allowing them decision-making power over their own education. At The Brooklyn Free School, students are required to show up for a minimum of 5½ hours per day, but what they do with that time is entirely up to them. The only mandatory activity is the weekly Democratic Meeting, set aside to solve problems and decide rules. Every attendee, from the youngest child to the most senior staff member, receives an equal vote. Students choose to participate in a wide range of holistic, educational activities, from listening to presidential press conferences to co-teaching science classes to completing a yoga practice.[13,14]

Free schools are one example of how to nurture childhood intention. While many of us might be unable to provide such significant freedoms (due to location, cost, and commitment to tradition, to name a few barriers), we can enact our version of the free school philosophy on a smaller scale and in our own way.

Attaching responsibilities to our children's freedoms is straight-forward and easy. They might be allowed to pick a television show to watch, but they also have to take into account the needs and limitations of their younger sibling, who will pick the next time. Implementing this philosophy in reverse, attaching freedoms to their responsibilities, is also important to try. If their role in the house is to do the dishes, for example, let them do it the way they think works best. Older children can be asked to make dinner once a week, with the freedom to make whatever they want, within limits, of course (looking at you chocolate, gummy bear, and sugar omelet!). Given both freedom and responsibility, children become far more capable, far more independent—and far more intentional.

In a work context, this may take the form of allowing a colleague to run with a project with minimal supervision, but holding them accountable for the results that they come up with. Too often in the interests of protecting our colleagues, otherwise skilled leaders restrict the freedom that they are sharing downward, and in doing so, limit their colleagues' speed of development.

STEP 3: GIVE A HELPFUL PUSH

Another way to inspire intentionality is forcing others to make decisions. One of the mistakes that we often make as leaders and parents is believing we must make decisions on behalf of those we're responsible for. While it may be the case occasionally, we can and should give others as much responsibility as they can handle. Even better, we should do it as early as possible, helping them to take ownership of their own intentions. The first step is acknowledging that they can and should be actively involved in decision-making to the limits of their capability. Then all that's left is giving them the chance to do so.

The best way to give kids the power of intention is to force them to make choices as soon as possible. Like anything else, there's a spectrum we can explore: we should stop our kids from crossing a busy street, but we don't need to pick their clothes. They can choose their own clothing as soon as they're old enough to point and process. Even in colder climates, where there is no real option sometimes, try to find opportunities for choice. Mandating that your young child wear snow pants ensures their health and safety, but the pants (or not!) that they wear under them are fair game.

This can be scary for a parent, but as long as you're limiting freedom to choices with minor consequences, there's little risk attached. Your child will benefit far more from experiencing independence and intention than they will from being "helicoptered." Children are better served making real decisions and experiencing negative consequences when they're young than experiencing those negative consequences for the first time when they're older. Not doing your homework is a less consequential decision in second grade than it is in the second year of university.

On the other end of the intimacy spectrum, giving more choice to employees has not been the trend. A lot of the science of management engineering (now known as management consulting) in the past 50 years has been focused on efficiency gains. Most of these came from standardization of processes. The foundation of standardization is the elimination of choice. On the assembly line, you don't get to decide where to put the headlamp. In fact, you're evaluated on the opposite—your ability to place the headlamp in the exact same way, every time, as quickly as possible. We believe that a large part of the feelings of disengagement and languishing we talk about throughout this book come from the loss of agency that standardization brings.

But just like in education, an alternative movement in business has begun to gain traction around the world, notably in France with major companies like Michelin and Carrefour.[15] "Corporate liberation" shares a similar philosophy with free schools—instead of devising a work plan, leaders ask employees to devise their own. Instead of solving blockages, leaders ask their employees how they plan to solve them—and provide the necessary support. Companies that have adopted a corporate liberation model have seen dramatic results: Decathlon allows its business units to design their organizational workflow in whatever way best suits their needs. Leaders became coaches instead of directors, warehouses began to fulfill their own orders, and teams set their own schedules.[16] In 2017 and 2018, Decathlon was France's No. 1 Great Place to Work.[17] Given the success of liberated corporate structures, the ability to take ownership over work will likely be key to solving our modern disengagement dilemma.

STEP 4: SUPPORT LONG-TERM THINKING

Strategy, at its root, is about making choices in the face of uncertainty. In a corporate context, when we give our colleagues the opportunity to make choices, pushing them to think through the longer-term consequences of their choices, we give them the necessary tools for strategic thinking.

The same is true for children. Children, as they get older and start to build their reasoning capacity, can be engaged in discussions about the short- and long-term consequences of their choices. A question to ask your kids when they're making a choice is what they would think of their decisions one year in the future. Steer clear of paralyzing them with analysis, but sensitize them to thinking multiple steps ahead. A friend of Mike's once asked his 17-year-old son, who wanted to get a tattoo, "What tattoo would you have gotten 7 years ago, when you were 10? Would you be happy with that now? Do you think you'll be happy with this one 7 years from now?" Realizing that he might not be happy walking around with Dora the Explorer permanently inked on himself, the son decided to wait a while before going under the needle.

Giving Up Power for a Good Cause

When we're responsible for others, assuming that we know what's best for them can be easy. We want to protect them from the potential downsides of their decisions. If our child wants to wear fairy wings to school, we might try to dissuade them due to the fear that they might be mocked or bullied. If a new employee wants to take on an initiative outside their role description, we might stop them because we worry that it will leave them with insufficient time for core responsibilities. But those around us, from the youngest child to the newest employee, have their own set of personal perspectives and desires. A big part of our responsibility as parents and leaders is to help them develop their own intention as they grow.

Whether it's letting our toddler wear their Halloween costume in April or letting our new employee initiate a spin-off project, releasing control over the people we're responsible for can be difficult. We must remember that the more agency and room for intentionality that we give those around us—in the form of intertwined freedom and responsibility—the more they have the chance to grow.

CHAPTER 30

The Garden of Intention

"Gardens are not made by singing 'Oh, how beautiful,' and sitting in the shade."

—Rudyard Kipling

When we started writing this book, we were certain that:

- ◆ Intention is a big topic to cover in a single book.
- ◆ It has never been more important for us to be intentional—as individuals, family and community members, colleagues, and leaders.

When something is both urgent and impossibly vast, your only choice is to approach it with the 80/20 principle—to try to capture the essence of a solution that is simultaneously imperfect and impactful. This is how we chose what we say about the five ingredients of intention in this book: willpower, curiosity, integrity, attention, and habits. In our research, every high performer we read about and spoke with exemplifies these five ingredients (to different degrees). Equally important to us is the compelling evidence that each of these ingredients is highly trainable—each of them, with intention, can be improved.

We started this book by talking about a problem that defines our modern era: despite doing collectively better in terms of many objective health and wellness measures, many of us (and often the most fortunate among us) live in a state of languish. As disengagement soars, leaving us to search for or create meaning in our personal and professional lives, we have come to rely on less satisfying substitutes for the depth of connection and purpose we yearn for and deserve. In a way, because we lack the proper nutrients of a true sense of meaning, we're drawn in by the junk food of substitutes and replacements. We fill our lives with tools and activities that have been designed to short-circuit our brains into feeling engaged, but which leave us starved for a true sense of agency and purpose.

Planting a Garden

As we've said previously, one way to understand the ingredients we've presented in this book is as part of a garden. Imagine something like this (except maybe better drawn):

- ◆ **Willpower—The Sunlight:** Sunlight is the driving force behind growth. It provides vital energy, nurturing and sustaining each plant through its development. Like sunlight, willpower is nonlimited—all we need to do is make sure we don't create shade that limits our plants' potentials. The key takeaways from this section of the book are that perceiving willpower as a limited resource is an illusion, and more importantly, an obstacle. High performers consistently exceed their perceived limits by applying mindful awareness—this also allows them to not only reach their goals but to help those around them drive toward shared goals.

◆ **Curiosity—The Water:** Water is essential, nurturing the garden and reviving it after a hot day of sun. In the same way, our curiosity is essential for us to expand and evolve. Curiosity revitalizes our minds, inviting growth and allowing us to explore new paths beyond our previous limits. The key takeaway from this section of the book is that curiosity can help create a deeper engagement with the world, allowing us to expand our horizons and adapt to change. Understanding, examining, and changing their beliefs as they go along, high performers are able to think freely and help others avoid groupthink in order to create more intentional interactions.

◆ **Integrity—The Seeds:** Our values are like seeds of unrealized potential. Seeds may seem insignificant at first, but they set the stage for growth. Each seed carries within it the potential for a specific result. They must be carefully chosen, meticulously planted, and nurtured. It's our job to know which seed leads to which plant and then decide which ones to plant. The key takeaways from this section of the book are that high performers are able to live more authentically by examining what values actually drive them and then aligning their actions with those core values. Because core values are often common denominators between very different groups of people, this also allows them to better understand others and foster high performance and intention in those around them.

◆ **Attention—The Soil:** The rich soil—alive with vibrant organic diversity—provides nutrients. It dictates what the plants will consume and how much they can grow. Like soil, attention is the world that we construct and choose to live in. Attention nurtures our minds and allows us to create new realities for ourselves and those around us. The key takeaway here is that attention is a spotlight we choose to shine on various aspects of the world, thereby constructing our own private reality in the process. High performers are able to tap into this process by overcoming distractions and building that reality in a mindful and goal-oriented manner, allowing them to navigate life with ease.

- **Habits—The Roots:** The network of roots that lies beneath the garden connects it to the earth, grounding it, providing nutrients, and allowing for stability. Just like roots, our habits give constancy and stability to our progress. And just like roots, they take a stronger and stronger hold over time, becoming more difficult to change. The key takeaways in this final section were that habits are like an autopilot we put on. High performers know this and apply deep intention at the moment a habit is created, because they understand that these are points of extreme leverage that can dictate their lives. Mindfully creating and rewiring habits allows high performers to achieve what might look impossible to those around them.

Becoming a Gardener

The one thing that's missing in our garden analogy is you: the gardener. Your job is to bring all of these ingredients together—intentionally. You need an idea of the type of garden you want to grow. You need to know which plants to nurture. You need to be constantly vigilant, protecting your garden from outside threats. Your top challenges may shift as your garden grows, as the seeds mature into plants and the roots get stronger. Abandoning your garden to grow wild will leave you without a harvest, just as living without intention won't yield the high performance you crave.

The more you work on your garden, the more you'll see the many fruits (accomplishments, nurturing relationships, personal satisfaction) of your labor. By combining these five ingredients you'll be able to reap the harvest of a happy and successful life. Perhaps more importantly, you'll be able to contribute in a meaningful way to the lives of those around you—the friends, family, and teams that rely on you.

Despite the pace and gravity of modern life, many of us have a better opportunity for a truly rewarding life than ever before. We are in an era defined by choice. We have the freedom, as well as the burden, to define ourselves—to grow our garden the way we want to, with intention.

Notes

Chapter 1

1. A note on survey data: to get a better sense of how everyday people viewed our core themes, we surveyed 700 North American employees. We've included our key findings so you can get a sense of what the wider public thinks about intention and its many facets. The most relevant and surprising findings from that survey are interspersed throughout the book in notes, like this one.

Chapter 2

1. Keyes, C. L. (2002). The mental health continuum: From languishing to flourishing in life. *Journal of Health and Social Behavior*, *43*(2), 207–222.
2. Grant, A. (2021, December 3). Feeling blah during the pandemic? It's called languishing. *New York Times*. https://www.nytimes.com/2021/04/19/well/mind/covid-mental-health-languishing.html.
3. Major depression: The impact on overall health. (n.d.). Blue Cross Blue Shield. https://www.bcbs.com/the-health-of-america/reports/major-depression-the-impact-overall-health.
4. Goodwin, R. D., Weinberger, A. H., Kim, J. H., Wu, M., & Galea, S. (2020). Trends in anxiety among adults in the United States, 2008–2018: Rapid increases among young adults. *Journal of Psychiatric Research*, *130*, 441–446.
5. Martinez-Ales, G., Hernandez-Calle, D., Khauli, N., & Keyes, K. M. (2020). Why are suicide rates increasing in the United States? Towards a multilevel reimagination of suicide prevention. *Behavioral Neurobiology of Suicide and Self Harm*, 1–23.
6. Purcell, J. (2014). Disengaging from engagement. *Human Resource Management Journal*, *24*(3), 241–254.

7. Kato, T. A., Kanba, S., & Teo, A. R. (2019). Hikikomori: Multi-dimensional understanding, assessment, and future international perspectives. *Psychiatry and Clinical Neurosciences, 73*(8), 427–440.
8. Poe, E. A. (2021). *The imp of the perverse.* Lindhardt og Ringhof.
9. Liang, L. (2022, February 25). The psychology behind "revenge bedtime procrastination." BBC. https://www.bbc.co.uk/worklife/article/20201123-the-psychology-behind-revenge-bedtime-procrastination.
10. Nauts, S., Kamphorst, B. A., Stut, W., De Ridder, D. T., & Anderson, J. H. (2019). The explanations people give for going to bed late: A qualitative study of the varieties of bedtime procrastination. *Behavioral Sleep Medicine, 17*(6), 753–762.
11. Gallup, Inc. (2023, July 10). Global Indicator: Employee Engagement—Gallup. Gallup.com. https://www.gallup.com/394373/indicator-employee-engagement.aspx.

Chapter 3

1. Koch, C. (2016). Does brain size matter? *Scientific American Mind, 27*(1), 22–25.
2. Tattersall, I., & Schwartz, J. H. (1999). Hominids and hybrids: The place of Neanderthals in human evolution. *Proceedings of the National Academy of Sciences, 96*(13), 7117–7119.
3. O'Madagain, C., & Tomasello, M. (2022). Shared intentionality, reason-giving and the evolution of human culture. *Philosophical Transactions of the Royal Society B, 377*(1843), 20200320.
4. Searle, J. R. (1990). *Collective intentions and actions. Intentions in communication.* PR Cohen, J. Morgan and ME Pollak.
5. For more on this, see De Waal, F. (2016). *Are we smart enough to know how smart animals are?* WW Norton & Company.

Chapter 4

1. Baumeister, R. F., & Brewer, L. E. (2012). Believing versus disbelieving in free will: Correlates and consequences. *Social and Personality Psychology Compass, 6*(10), 736–745.
2. Frankl, V. E. (1985). *Man's search for meaning.* Simon and Schuster.

3. De Charms, R. (2013). *Personal causation: The internal affective determinants of behavior.* Routledge.

4. Cornudella Gaya, M. (2017). Autotelic principle: the role of intrinsic motivation in the emergence and development of artificial language. Doctoral dissertation, Paris Sciences et Lettres (ComUE), p. 39.

5. Frankfurt, H. G. (1988). *The importance of what we care about: Philosophical essays.* Cambridge University Press.

6. Gilbert, M. (1990). Walking together: A paradigmatic social phenomenon. *Midwest Studies in Philosophy, 15*(1), 1–14.

7. World Economic Forum. (2020). The Future of Jobs Report 2020. Retrieved from http://www3.weforum.org/docs/WEF_Future_of_Jobs_2020.pdf.

8. Chiang, T. (2023, May 4). Will A.I. Become the New McKinsey? *The New Yorker.* https://www.newyorker.com/science/annals-of-artificial-intelligence/will-ai-become-the-new-mckinsey.

Chapter 5

1. Simonsmeier, B. A., Andronie, M., Buecker, S., & Frank, C. (2021). The effects of imagery interventions in sports: A meta-analysis. *International Review of Sport and Exercise Psychology, 14*(1), 186–207.

2. Sport Imagery Training/Association for Applied Sport Psychology. (n.d.). https://appliedsportpsych.org/resources/resources-for-athletes/sport-imagery-training/.

3. See note 1.

4. Robbins, S. B., Lauver, K., Le, H., Davis, D., Langley, R., & Carlstrom, A. (2004). Do psychosocial and study skill factors predict college outcomes? A meta-analysis. *Psychological Bulletin, 130*(2), 261.

5. Mann, T., Tomiyama, A. J., Westling, E., Lew, A. M., Samuels, B., & Chatman, J. (2007). Medicare's search for effective obesity treatments: Diets are not the answer. *American Psychologist, 62*(3), 220.

6. Davison, J. M., Share, M., Hennessy, M., & Stewart-Knox, B. J. (2015). Caught in a "spiral": Barriers to healthy eating and dietary health promotion needs from the perspective of unemployed young people and their service providers. *Appetite, 85*, 146–154.

7. Savelli, E., & Murmura, F. (2023). The intention to consume healthy food among older Gen-Z: Examining antecedents and mediators. *Food Quality and Preference, 105,* 104788.

Chapter 6

1. Baumeister, R. F., Bratslavsky, E., Muraven, M., & Tice, D. M. (1998). Ego depletion: Is the active self a limited resource? *Journal of Personality and Social Psychology, 74*(5), 1252–1265.
2. Xu, H., Bègue, L., & Bushman, B. J. (2012). Too fatigued to care: Ego depletion, guilt, and prosocial behavior. *Journal of Experimental Social Psychology, 48*(5), 1183–1186.
3. Baumeister, R. F. (2003). Ego depletion and self-regulation failure: A resource model of self-control. Alcoholism. *Clinical and Experimental Research, 27*(2), 281–284.
4. Dorris, D. C., Power, D. A., & Kenefick, E. (2012). Investigating the effects of ego depletion on physical exercise routines of athletes. *Psychology of Sport and Exercise, 13*(2), 118–125.
5. Miller, H. C., DeWall, C. N., Pattison, K., Molet, M., & Zentall, T. R. (2012). Too dog tired to avoid danger: Self-control depletion in canines increases behavioral approach toward an aggressive threat. *Psychonomic Bulletin & Review,* 19, 535–540.
6. Englert, C., & Bertrams, A. (2021). Again, no evidence for or against the existence of ego depletion: Opinion on "A multi-site preregistered paradigmatic test of the ego depletion effect." *Frontiers in Human Neuroscience, 15,* 658890.
7. Engber, D. (2016).Everything is Crumbling. Slate Magazine. http://www.slate.com/articles/health_and_science/cover_ story/2016/03/ego_depletion_an_influential_theory_in_psycho logy_may_have_just_been_debunked.html?wpsrc=sh_all_ dt_tw_top.
8. Job, V., Dweck, C. S., & Walton, G. M. (2010). Ego depletion—Is it all in your head? Implicit theories about willpower affect self-regulation. *Psychological Science, 21*(11), 1686–1693.
9. Job, V., Walton, G. M., Bernecker, K., & Dweck, C. S. (2015). Implicit theories about willpower predict self-regulation and

grades in everyday life. *Journal of Personality and Social Psychology, 108*(4), 637.

10. Compagnoni, M., Sieber, V., & Job, V. (2020). My brain needs a break: Kindergarteners' willpower theories are related to behavioral self-regulation. *Frontiers in Psychology*, 3567.

11. Goggins, D. (2021). *Can't hurt me: Master your mind and defy the odds*. Lioncrest Publishers.

12. Powell, A. (2018). Ellen Langer's state of mindfulness. *The Harvard Gazette*. Boston: Harvard University.

13. Miller, E. M., Walton, G. M., Dweck, C. S., Job, V., Trzesniewski, K. H., & McClure, S. M. (2012). Theories of willpower affect sustained learning. *PloS One, 7*(6), e38680.

Chapter 7

1. Snider, B. (2012). The life of Warren "Batso" Harding. Climbing. https://www.climbing.com/people/the-life-of-warren-andquot-batsoandquot-harding/.

2. Horst, E. (2010). *Maximum climbing: mental training for peak performance and optimal experience*. Rowman & Littlefield.

3. Margaritoff, M. (2023). The true story of Dashrath Manjhi—India's beloved "Mountain Man." All That's Interesting. https://allthatsinteresting.com/dashrath-manjhi.

4. Magen, E., & Gross, J. J. (2007). Harnessing the need for immediate gratification: Cognitive reconstrual modulates the reward value of temptations. *Emotion, 7*(2), 415.

5. Gross, J. (2023, March 15). Personal communication. [Personal interview].

6. Again, this is not to imply that there are no physical limitations—which may be a consequence of disease, differences in ability, and so on, but rather that our minds impose limitations that sometimes exceed our physical ones.

7. https://resources.soundstrue.com/michael-singer-podcast/.

8. Lutz, A., Slagter, H. A., Dunne, J. D., & Davidson, R. J. (2008). Attention regulation and monitoring in meditation. *Trends in Cognitive Sciences, 12*(4), 163–169.

Chapter 8

1. Gibson, E. L., & Green, M. W. (2002). Nutritional influences on cognitive function: mechanisms of susceptibility. *Nutrition Research Reviews, 15*(1), 169–206.

2. Lennie, P. (2003). The cost of cortical computation. *Current Biology, 13*(6), 493–497. Messier, C. (2004). Glucose improvement of memory: A review. *European Journal of Pharmacology, 490*(1–3), 33–57.

3. Gibson, E. L. (2007). Carbohydrates and mental function: Feeding or impeding the brain? *Nutrition Bulletin, 32*, 71–83.

4. Clarke, D. D. (1999). Circulation and energy metabolism of the brain. *Basic Neurochemistry: Molecular, Cellular, and Medical Aspects.* Clarke, D. D., Sokoloff, L. (1999). Circulation and energy metabolism of the brain. In Siegel, G. J., Agranoff, B. W., Albers, R. W., et al. (eds.), *Basic neurochemistry: Molecular, cellular and medical aspects.* 6th edition, Chapter 31. Philadelphia: Lippincott-Raven. Available from https://www.ncbi.nlm.nih.gov/books/NBK20413/.

5. Job, V., Walton, G. M., Bernecker, K., & Dweck, C. S. (2013). Beliefs about willpower determine the impact of glucose on self-control. *Proceedings of the National Academy of Sciences of the United States of America, 110*(37), 14837–14842.

6. See note 5.

7. The costs of insufficient sleep. (n.d.). RAND. https://www.rand.org/randeurope/research/projects/the-value-of-the-sleep-economy.html.

8. See note 7.

9. Rivkin, W., Diestel, S., Stollberger, J., & Sacramento, C. (2023). The role of regulatory, affective, and motivational resources in the adverse spillover of sleep in the home domain to employee effectiveness in the work domain. *Human Relations, 76*(2), 199–232.

10. Rivkin, W. (2023, March 5). Personal communication [Personal interview].

11. Goggins, D. (2021). *Can't hurt me: Master your mind and defy the odds.* Lioncrest.

12. Cheung, B. Y., Takemura, K., Ou, C., Gale, A., & Heine, S. J. (2021). Considering cross-cultural differences in sleep duration

between Japanese and Canadian university students. *PloS One*, *16*(4), e0250671.

13. Brewer, J. (2023, March 31). Personal communication [Personal interview].

14. See note 13.

15. See note 13.

Chapter 9

1. Camparo, S., Maymin, P. Z., Park, C., Yoon, S., Zhang, C., Lee, Y., & Langer, E. J. (2022). The fatigue illusion: The physical effects of mindlessness. *Humanities and Social Sciences Communications*, *9*(1), 1–16.

2. Langer, E. J. (1989). *Mindfulness*. Reading, MA: Addison-Wesley Pub. Co.

3. See note 1.

4. Langer, E. J. (1989). *Mindfulness*. Reading, MA: Addison-Wesley Pub. Co., 234.

5. Chiesa, A., Calati, R., & Serretti, A. (2011). Does mindfulness training improve cognitive abilities? A systematic review of neuropsychological findings. *Clinical Psychology Review*, *31*(3), 449–464.

6. Davenport, C., & Pagnini, F. (2016). Mindful learning: A case study of Langerian mindfulness in schools. *Frontiers in Psychology*, 7, 1372.

7. Creswell, J. D. (2017). Mindfulness interventions. *Annual Review of Psychology*, *68*, 491–516.

8. Pagnini, F., Phillips, D., Bercovitz, K., & Langer, E. (2019). Mindfulness and relaxation training for long duration spaceflight: Evidences from analog environments and military settings. *Acta Astronautica*, *165*, 1–8.

9. Pagnini, F., Bercovitz, K., & Langer, E. (2016). Perceived control and mindfulness: Implications for clinical practice. *Journal of Psychotherapy Integration*, *26*(2), 91.

10. Amabile, T., & Kramer, S. (2011). *The progress principle: Using small wins to ignite joy, engagement, and creativity at work*. Harvard Business Press.

11. Amabile, T., & Kramer, S. The power of small wins. *Harvard Business Review*. https://hbr.org/2011/05/the-power-of-small-wins.
12. Ryan, R. M., & Deci, E. L. (2000). Self-determination theory and the facilitation of intrinsic motivation, social development, and well-being. *American Psychologist, 55*(1), 68.
13. Krakovsky, M. (2012). The secrets of self-improvement. *Scientific American Mind, 23*(1), 38–43. https://doi.org/10.1038/scientificamericanmind0312-38.
14. Bishop, K. (2022, February 25). Why relying on productivity tools can backfire. BBC Worklife. https://www.bbc.com/worklife/article/20210208-why-relying-on-productivity-tools-can-backfire.
15. Dunn, J. (2023, June 30). Me walk pretty one day. *New York Times*. https://www.nytimes.com/2023/06/30/well/david-sedaris-walking.html.
16. Salerno, A., Laran, J., & Janiszewski, C. (2015). Pride and regulatory behavior: The influence of appraisal information and self-regulatory goals. *Journal of Consumer Research, 42*(3), 499–514.

Chapter 10

1. Smith, P. (2016, May 3). Leicester City win Premier League: How they did it differently. Sky Sports. https://www.skysports.com/football/news/30385/10267972/leicester-win-premier-league-how-they-did-it-differently.
2. Christakis, N. A., & Fowler, J. H. (2008). The collective dynamics of smoking in a large social network. *New England Journal of Medicine, 358*(21), 2249–2258.
3. Borsari, Brian, & Kate B. Carey. (2001). Peer influences on college drinking: A review of the research. *Journal of Substance Abuse, 13*(4), 391–424.
4. Farrow, K., Grolleau, G., & Ibanez, L. (2017). Social norms and pro-environmental behavior: A review of the evidence. *Ecological Economics, 140*, 1–13.
5. Bandura, A. (2000). Exercise of human agency through collective efficacy. *Current Directions in Psychological Science, 9*(3), 75–78.

6. Linnenluecke, M. K., Verreynne, M., Scheepers, M., & Venter, C. (2017). A review of collaborative planning approaches for transformative change toward a sustainable future. *Journal of Cleaner Production*, *142*, 3212–3224. https://doi.org/10.1016/j .jclepro.2016.10.148.

7. Wang, D., Waldman, D. A., & Zhang, Z. (2014). A meta-analysis of shared leadership and team effectiveness. *Journal of Applied Psychology*, *99*(2), 181.

8. Zhao, Z., & Hou, J. (2009). The study on psychological capital development of intrapreneurial team. *International Journal of Psychological Studies*, *1*(2), 35–40.

9. Bai, Y., Feng, Z., & Job, V. (2022). Performance benefits of employees' own and their coworkers' nonlimited willpower beliefs. In *Academy of Management Proceedings*, *2022*(1), 11380). Briarcliff Manor, NY: Academy of Management.

10. Rock, D., & Grant, H. (2016). Why diverse teams are smarter. *Harvard Business Review*, *4*(4), 2–5.

11. See note 9.

Chapter 11

1. Silberman, S. (2015). *Neurotribes: The legacy of autism and the future of neurodiversity*. Penguin.

2. Bernard, R. Foreword. In Grandin, T., & Scariano, M. (1986). *Emergence: labeled autistic*. Novato, CA: Arena Press.

3. Loewenstein, G. (1994). The psychology of curiosity: A review and reinterpretation. *Psychological Bulletin*, *116*(1), 75.

4. Padulo, C., Marascia, E., Conte, N., Passarello, N., Mandolesi, L., & Fairfield, B. (2022). Curiosity killed the cat but not memory: Enhanced performance in high-curiosity states. *Brain Sciences*, *12*(7), 846.

5. Galli, G., Sirota, M., Gruber, M. J., Ivanof, B. E., Ganesh, J., Materassi, M., . . . & Craik, F. I. (2018). Learning facts during aging: The benefits of curiosity. *Experimental Aging Research*, *44*(4), 311–328.

6. Kashdan, T. B., & Yuen, M. (2007). Whether highly curious students thrive academically depends on the learning environment of their school: A study of Hong Kong adolescents. *Motivation and Emotion*, *31*(4), 260–270.

7. Gallagher, M. W., & Lopez, S. J. (2007). Curiosity and well-being. *Journal of Positive Psychology, 2,* 236–248.

8. Sharp, E. S., Reynolds, C. A., Pedersen, N. L., & Gatz, M. (2010). Cognitive engagement and cognitive aging: Is openness protective? *Psychology and Aging, 25*(1), 60.

9. Kashdan, T. B., & Steger, M. F. (2007). Curiosity and pathways to wellbeing and meaning in life: Traits, states, and everyday behaviors. *Motivation and Emotion, 31,* 159–173.

10. Mussel, P. (2013). Introducing the construct curiosity for predicting job performance. *Journal of Organizational Behavior, 34*(4), 453–472.

11. Graham, P. (2019). The Bus Ticket Theory of Genius. http://www.paulgraham.com/genius.html.

12. Ziegler, M., Cengia, A., Mussel, P., & Gerstorf, D. (2015). Openness as a buffer against cognitive decline: The Openness-Fluid-Crystallized-Intelligence (OFCI) model applied to late adulthood. *Psychology and Aging, 30*(3), 573–588. https://doi.org/10.1037/a0039493.

13. Sakaki, M., Yagi, A., & Murayama, K. (2018b). Curiosity in old age: A possible key to achieving adaptive aging. *Neuroscience & Biobehavioral Reviews, 88,* 106–116. https://doi.org/10.1016/j.neubiorev.2018.03.007.

14. Setiya, K. (2023, April 4). Personal communication [Personal interview].

15. See note 14.

16. How philosophy can solve your midlife crisis. (2017, October 2). MIT News. Massachusetts Institute of Technology. https://news.mit.edu/2017/how-philosophy-can-solve-your-midlife-crisis-1003.

17. See note 14.

Chapter 12

1. Ma, Y., Dixon, G., & Hmielowski, J. D. (2019). Psychological reactance from reading basic facts on climate change: The role of prior views and political identification. *Environmental Communication, 13*(1), 71–86.

2. Kahan, D. M. (2013). Ideology, motivated reasoning, and cognitive reflection. *Judgment and Decision Making, 8*(4), 407–424.

3. Housel, M. (2023, March 29). Mental liquidity. Collab Fund. https://collabfund.com/blog/mental-liquidity/.

4. Santana, A. N., Roazzi, A., & de Nobre, A. P. M. C. (2022). The relationship between cognitive flexibility and mathematical performance in children: A meta-analysis. *Trends in Neuroscience and Education*, September 28: 100179. doi: 10.1016/j.tine.2022.100179. Epub 2022 Apr 30. PMID: 35999015.

5. Colé, P., Duncan, L. G., & Blaye, A. (2014). Cognitive flexibility predicts early reading skills. *Frontiers in Psychology, 5*, 565.

6. Kalia, V., Fuesting, M., & Cody, M. (2019). Perseverance in solving Sudoku: Role of grit and cognitive flexibility in problem solving. *Journal of Cognitive Psychology, 31*(3), 370–378.

7. Smith, C. A., & Konik, J. (2022). Who is satisfied with life? Personality, cognitive flexibility, and life satisfaction. *Current Psychology, 41*(12), 9019–9026.

8. Legare, C. H., Dale, M. T., Kim, S. Y., & Deák, G. O. (2018). Cultural variation in cognitive flexibility reveals diversity in the development of executive functions. *Scientific Reports, 8*(1), 1–14.

9. Diamond, A., & Lee, K. (2011). Interventions shown to aid executive function development in children 4 to 12 years old. *Science, 333*(6045), 959–964.

10. Karbach, J., & Kray, J. (2009). How useful is executive control training? Age differences in near and far transfer of task-switching training. *Developmental Science, 12*(6), 978–990.

Chapter 13

1. This frustration with a "post-truth" world is, ironically, symptomatic of the same Belief stickiness. The Belief that being rational is "good" and that a rational person integrates all information that "official" sources throw their way, is very much a Belief and not a cold-hard fact. Real humans make decisions in far more nuanced ways, as research on topics such as vaccine hesitancy has shown. But that's another story.

2. Demetrious, K. (2022). Deep canvassing: Persuasion, ethics, democracy and activist public relations. *Public Relations Inquiry,* *11*(3), 361–377.

3. Kalla, J. L., & Broockman, D. E. (2020). Reducing exclusionary attitudes through interpersonal conversation: Evidence from three field experiments. *American Political Science Review,* *114*(2), 410–425.

4. Why is it so hard to change people's minds? (n.d.). Greater Good. https://greatergood.berkeley.edu/article/item/why_is_it_ so_hard_to_change_peoples_minds.

Chapter 14

1. Asch, S. E. (1951). Effects of group pressure upon the modification and distortion of judgments. *Groups, Leadership, and Men,* 177–190.

2. Example cards from the Asch experiment. Wikipedia contributors. (2023). Asch conformity experiments. Wikipedia. https://en .wikipedia.org/wiki/Asch_conformity_experiments.

3. Asch, S. (1955). Opinions and social pressure. *Scientific American, 193*(5), 31–35.

4. Bahrami, B., Olsen, K., Latham, P. E., Roepstorff, A., Rees, G., & Frith, C. D. (2010). Optimally interacting minds. *Science, 329*(5995), 1081–1085.

5. Bahrami, B. (2023, May 23). Personal communication [Personal interview].

6. Janis, I. L. (1972). *Victims of Groupthink: A Psychological Study of Foreign-policy Decisions and Fiascoes.* Houghton Mifflin.

7. Janis, I. L. (1982). *Groupthink.* (2nd ed.). Boston: Houghton Mifflin.

8. What caused the *Challenger* disaster? (2022, January 28). HISTORY. https://www.history.com/news/how-the-challenger-disaster-changed-nasa.

9. House Committee. (1986). Investigation of the Challenger accident: report of the Committee on Science and Technology, House of Representatives, Ninety-ninth Congress. Second session, 4.

10. Schwartz, J., & Wald, M. L. (2003, March 9). The Nation: NASA's curse? "Groupthink" is 30 years old, and still going strong.

New York Times. https://www.nytimes.com/2003/03/09/weekinreview/the-nation-nasa-s-curse-groupthink-is-30-years-old-and-still-going-strong.html.

11. See note 5, p. 89.

12. Edmondson, A. (1999). Psychological safety and learning behavior in work teams. *Administrative Science Quarterly, 44*(2), 350–383.

13. Edmonson, A.C. (2023, April 1). Personal communication [Personal interview].

14. Edmondson, A. C. (2018). *The fearless organization: Creating psychological safety in the workplace for learning, innovation, and growth.* John Wiley & Sons.

Chapter 15

1. Junod, T. (2022, December 23). Mister Rogers's enduring wisdom. *The Atlantic.* https://www.theatlantic.com/magazine/archive/2019/12/what-would-mister-rogers-do/600772/.

2. Higgins, C. (2012, August 4). Mister Rogers' epic 9-part, 4.5-hour interview/Mental Floss. Mental Floss. https://www.mentalfloss.com/article/31389/mister-rogers-epic-9-part-45-hour-interview.

3. Brooks, D. (2015, April 11). Opinion/The moral bucket list. *New York Times.* https://www.nytimes.com/2015/04/12/opinion/sunday/david-brooks-the-moral-bucket-list.html.

4. Ashoka Biography. (2019, July 25). Biography Online. https://www.biographyonline.net/royalty/ashoka-biography.html.

Chapter 16

1. Branson, C. M. (2008, May 9). Achieving organisational change through values alignment. *Journal of Educational Administration, 46*(3), 376–395.

2. Witteman, H. O., Ndjaboue, R., Vaisson, G., Dansokho, S. C., Arnold, B., Bridges, J. F., . . . & Jansen, J. (2021). Clarifying values: An updated and expanded systematic review and meta-analysis. *Medical Decision Making, 41*(7), 801–820.

3. Bostrom, N. (2003). Ethical issues in advanced artificial intelligence. *Science Fiction and Philosophy: From Time Travel to Superintelligence,* 277, 284.

4. Schwartz, S. H., & Bilsky, W. (1987). Toward a universal psychological structure of human values. *Journal of Personality and Social Psychology, 53*(3), 551.

5. Fritz, M. R., & Guthrie, K. L. (2017). Values clarification: Essential for leadership learning. *Journal of Leadership Education, 16*(1), 47–63.

6. Toyota Motor Asia Pacific Pte Ltd. (2006, March). Ask "why" five times about every matter. Toyota Myanmar. Retrieved November 27, 2022, from https://web.archive.org/web/20221127052017/https://www.toyota-myanmar.com/about-toyota/toyota-traditions/quality/ask-why-five-times-about-every-matter.

7. Bicchieri, C., Muldoon, R., & Sontuoso, A. (2014). Social norms. *The Stanford Encyclopedia of Philosophy.*

8. Barrett, L. F. (2017). *How emotions are made: The secret life of the brain.* Pan Macmillan.

9. Wenglinsky, M. (1975). Obedience to Authority: An Experimental View. *Contemporary Sociology: A Journal of Reviews, 47*(4).

10. Loveday, P. M., Lovell, G. P., & Jones, C. M. (2018). The best possible selves intervention: A review of the literature to evaluate efficacy and guide future research. *Journal of Happiness Studies, 19*, 607–628.

Chapter 17

1. Schwartz, S. J., Côté, J. E., & Arnett, J. J. (2005). Identity and agency in emerging adulthood: Two developmental routes in the individualization process. *Youth and Society, 37*(2), 201–229.

2. Greene, J. D., Nystrom, L. E., Engell, A. D., Darley, J. M., & Cohen, J. D. (2004). The neural bases of cognitive conflict and control in moral judgment. *Neuron, 44*(2), 389–400.

3. Haidt, J., & Graham, J. (2007). When morality opposes justice: Conservatives have moral intuitions that liberals may not recognize. *Social Justice Research, 20*(1), 98–116.

4. Giles, L. C., Glonek, G., Luszcz, M. A., & Andrews, G. R. (2005). Effect of social networks on 10 year survival in very old Australians: The Australian longitudinal study of aging. *Journal of Epidemiology and Community Health, 59*(7), 574–579.

5. Hassan, J. (2021, June 1). Naomi Osaka hailed for bravery, pilloried for "diva behavior" amid French Open withdrawal. *Washington Post.* https://www.washingtonpost.com/world/2021/06/01/naomi-osaka-world-reacts-mental-health/.

6. Image from Duarte, N. (2013). *Resonate: Present visual stories that transform audiences.* John Wiley & Sons, 77.

7. Heyward, G. (2023, January 11). Naomi Osaka announces pregnancy and plans to return to tennis. NPR. https://www.npr.org/2023/01/11/1148411161/naomi-osaka-pregnant-baby-tennis-return.

8. Randel, A. E., Galvin, B. M., Shore, L. M., Ehrhart, K. H., Chung, B. G., Dean, M. A., & Kedharnath, U. (2018). Inclusive leadership: Realizing positive outcomes through belongingness and being valued for uniqueness. *Human Resource Management Review*, *28*(2), 190--03.

9. Schulz-Hardt, S., Brodbeck, F. C., Mojzisch, A., Kerschreiter, R., & Frey, D. (2006). Group decision making in hidden profile situations: dissent as a facilitator for decision quality. *Journal of Personality and Social Psychology*, *91*(6), 1080.

10. Lee, H., An, S., Lim, G. Y., & Sohn, Y. W. (2021). Ethical leadership and followers' emotional exhaustion: Exploring the roles of three types of emotional labor toward leaders in South Korea. *International Journal of Environmental Research and Public Health*, *18*(20), 10862.

Chapter 18

1. Tuckman, B. W. (1965). Developmental sequence in small groups. *Psychological Bulletin*, *63*(6), 384.

2. Pronin, E., Kruger, J., Savtisky, K., & Ross, L. (2001). You don't know me, but I know you: The illusion of asymmetric insight. *Journal of Personality and Social Psychology*, *81*(4), 639.

3. Pronin, E., Kruger, J., Savtisky, K., & Ross, L. (2001). You don't know me, but I know you: The illusion of asymmetric insight. *Journal of Personality and Social Psychology*, *81*(4), 639, 647.

4. Ames, D. R. (2004). Inside the mind reader's tool kit: projection and stereotyping in mental state inference. *Journal of Personality and Social Psychology*, *87*(3), 340.

5. Tamir, D. I., & Mitchell, J. P. (2013). Anchoring and adjustment during social inferences. *Journal of Experimental Psychology: General, 142*(1), 151–162.

6. Ames, D. R. (2004). Inside the mind reader's tool kit: Projection and stereotyping in mental state inference. *Journal of Personality and Social Psychology, 87*(3), 340.

7. Tappin, B. M., & McKay, R. T. (2017). The illusion of moral superiority. *Social Psychological and Personality Science, 8*(6), 623–631.

8. Similar to those studies that found that 80% of drivers think they are above-average drivers.

9. Extrinsic incentive bias—The Decision Lab. (n.d.). The Decision Lab. https://thedecisionlab.com/biases/extrinsic-incentive-bias.

10. Silvia, P. J. (2021). The self-reflection and insight scale: Applying item response theory to craft an efficient short form. *Current Psychology.* https://doi.org/10.1007/s12144-020-01299-7.

11. Carr, S. E., & Johnson, P. H. (2013). Does self-reflection and insight correlate with academic performance in medical students? *BMC Med Educ., 13*(1), 113–126.

12. Baghramian, M., Petherbridge, D., & Stout, R. (2020). Vulnerability and trust: An introduction. *International Journal of Philosophical Studies, 28*(5), 575–582.

13. Lencioni, P. (2002). *The five dysfunctions of a team: A leadership fable.* Jossey-Bass. https://www.amazon.ca/Five-Dysfunctions-Team-Leadership-Fable/dp/0787960756.

14. Many studies have shown that folks that have contact with other groups in a society are less likely to be prejudiced or racist against those other groups. For example, Pettigrew, T. F., & Tropp, L. R. (2006). A meta-analytic test of intergroup contact theory. *Journal of Personality and Social Psychology, 90*(5), 751.

15. Adapted from a list by James Clear, who says that he was inspired in turn by work he did with The LeaderShape Institute.

Chapter 19

1. Dawson, B. C. (2024, May 24). Kiichiro and Eiji Toyoda: Blazing the Toyota Way. BW Online. https://web.archive.org/

web/20100124180127/http://www.businessweek.com/magazine/content/04_21/b3884031_mz072.htm.

2. Burry, M. J. (2010, April 3). Opinion. I saw the crisis coming. Why didn't the Fed? *New York Times.* https://www.nytimes.com/2010/04/04/opinion/04burry.html.

3. Epictetus. *Enchiridion.* Translated by George Long. Dover Publications, 2004.

4. For more on the cola wars, see Louis, J. C., & Yazijian, H. Z. (1980). *The Cola Wars.* Everest House.

Chapter 20

1. Eriksen, C. W., & Yeh, Y. Y. (1985). Allocation of attention in the visual field. *Journal of Experimental Psychology: Human Perception and Performance, 11*(5), 583.

2. Ireland, J. D. (2007). *Udana and the Itivuttaka: Two classics from the Pali Canon* (Vol. 214). Buddhist Publication Society.

3. Affect Heuristic—The Decision Lab. (n.d.). The Decision Lab. https://thedecisionlab.com/biases/affect-heuristic.

4. The Impact of Gratitude on Mental Health—NAMI California. (2021, January 8). NAMI California. https://namica.org/blog/the-impact-of-gratitude-on-mental-health/.

5. Wong, Y. J., Owen, J., Gabana, N. T., Brown, J. W., McInnis, S., Toth, P., & Gilman, L. (2018). Does gratitude writing improve the mental health of psychotherapy clients? Evidence from a randomized controlled trial. *Psychotherapy Research, 28*(2), 192–202.

6. Mendelson, A. (2001). Effects of Novelty in News Photographs on Attention and Memory. *Media Psychology, 3*(2), 119–157.

7. Harris, R. (2019). Defining and measuring the productive office. *Journal of Corporate Real Estate, 21*(1), 55–71.

8. Locke, E. A., & Latham, G. P. (2002). Building a practically useful theory of goal setting and task motivation: A 35-year odyssey. *American Psychologist, 57*(9), 705.

9. Locke, E. A., & Bryan, J. (1969). The directing function of goals in task performance. *Organizational Behavior and Human Performance, 4,* 35–42.

Chapter 21

1. Wood, R. C., Levine, D. S., Cory, G. A., & Wilson, D. R. (2015). Evolutionary neuroscience and motivation in organizations. In *Organizational neuroscience* (Vol. 7, pp. 143–167). Emerald Group Publishing Limited.

2. Elliot, A. J., & McGregor, H. A. (2001). A 2×2 achievement goal framework. *Journal of Personality and Social Psychology*, *80*(3), 501.

3. Howell, A. J., & Watson, D. C. (2007). Procrastination: Associations with achievement goal orientation and learning strategies. *Personality and Individual Differences*, *43*(1), 167–178.

4. Wang, H., & Lehman, J. D. (2021). Using achievement goal-based personalized motivational feedback to enhance online learning. *Educational Technology Research and Development*, *69*, 553–581.

Chapter 22

1. Zabelina, D. L., O'Leary, D., Pornpattananangkul, N., Nusslock, R., & Beeman, M. (2015). Creativity and sensory gating indexed by the P50: Selective versus leaky sensory gating in divergent thinkers and creative achievers. *Neuropsychologia*, *69*, 77–84.

2. Zabelina, D., Saporta, A., & Beeman, M. (2016). Flexible or leaky attention in creative people? Distinct patterns of attention for different types of creative thinking. *Memory & Cognition*, *44*, 488–498.

3. Dirlewanger M, et al. (2000). Effects of short-term carbohydrate or fat overfeeding on energy expenditure and plasma leptin concentrations in healthy female subjects. *Int J Obes Relat Metab Disord*, *24*(11): 1413–8. doi:10.1038/sj.ijo.0801395.

4. Kuijer, R. G., & Boyce, J. A. (2014). Chocolate cake. Guilt or celebration? Associations with healthy eating attitudes, perceived behavioural control, intentions and weight-loss. *Appetite*, *74*, 48–54.

5. Bandura, A. (1997). *Self-efficacy: The exercise of control*. New York: W.H. Freeman.

6. Dweck, C. S. (2006). *Mindset: The new psychology of success*. New York: Random House.

Chapter 23

1. Csíkszentmihályi, M. (2000). *Beyond boredom and anxiety.* Jossey-Bass.
2. Nakamura, J., & Csíkszentmihályi, M. (2009). Flow theory and research. *Handbook of positive psychology, 195,* 206.
3. Barrett, N. F. (2011). "Wuwei" and flow: Comparative reflections on spirituality, transcendence, and skill in the Zhuangzi. *Philosophy East and West,* 679–706. https://www.jstor.org/stable/23015337.
4. Thatcher, A., Wretschko, G., & Fridjhon, P. (2008). Online flow experiences, problematic Internet use and Internet procrastination. *Computers in Human Behavior, 24*(5), 2236–2254.
5. Harari, Y. N. (2008). Combat flow: Military, political, and ethical dimensions of subjective well-being in war. *Review of General Psychology, 12*(3), 253–264.
6. See note 5.
7. Dixon, M. J., Stange, M., Larche, C. J., Graydon, C., Fugelsang, J. A., & Harrigan, K. A. (2018). Dark flow, depression and multiline slot machine play. *Journal of Gambling Studies, 34,* 73–-84.
8. Aust, F., Beneke, T., Peifer, C., & Wekenborg, M. (2022). The relationship between flow experience and burnout symptoms: A systematic review. *International Journal of Environmental Research and Public Health, 19,* 3865. https://doi.org/10.3390/ijerph19073865.
9. See note 8.
10. Vallerand, R. J. (2015). *The psychology of passion: A dualistic model.* Series in Positive Psychology.
11. Zumeta, L. N., Oriol, X., Telletxea, S., Amutio, A., & Basabe, N. (2016). Collective efficacy in sports and physical activities: Perceived emotional synchrony and shared flow. *Frontiers in Psychology, 6,* 1960.
12. van den Hout, J. J., & Davis, O. C. (2022). Promoting the emergence of team flow in organizations. *International Journal of Applied Positive Psychology, 7*(2), 143–189.

Chapter 24

1. Schulz-Hardt, S., Brodbeck, F. C., Mojzisch, A., Kerschreiter, R., & Frey, D. (2006). Group decision making in hidden profile situations: dissent as a facilitator for decision quality. *Journal of Personality and Social Psychology, 91*(6), 1080.
2. De Dreu, C. K., & West, M. A. (2001). Minority dissent and team innovation: The importance of participation in decision making. *Journal of Applied Psychology, 86*(6), 1191.
3. Massachusetts Institute of Technology. (2018, April 9). Morela, H. The Impossibility of Focusing on Two Things at Once. *MIT Sloan Management Review.* https://sloanreview.mit.edu/article/the-impossibility-of-focusing-on-two-things-at-once/#:~:text=Neurological%20science%20has%20demonstrated%20that,on%20two%20things%20at%20once.
4. Why Multitasking Doesn't Work. (2022, October 11). Cleveland Clinic. https://health.clevelandclinic.org/science-clear-multitasking-doesnt-work/#:~:text=We're%20really%20wired%20to,doing%20two%20things%20at%20once.
5. Larson, J. R., Jr., Foster-Fishman, P. G., & Keys, C. B. (1994). Discussion of shared and unshared information in decision-making groups. *Journal of Personality and Social Psychology, 67*(3), 446–461.

Chapter 25

1. Clear, J. (2018). *Atomic habits: An easy & proven way to build good habits & break bad ones.* Penguin.

Chapter 26

1. Wood, W., Quinn, J. M., & Kashy, D. A. (2002). Habits in everyday life: thought, emotion, and action. *Journal of Personality and Social Psychology, 83*(6), 1281.
2. Bargh, J. (1994). The four horsemen of automaticity: Awareness, intention, efficiency and control in social cognition. *Handbook of social cognition: Basic processes.* Erlbaum. 1–40.
3. Adriaanse, M. A., Kroese, F. M., Gillebaart, M., & De Ridder, D. T. (2014). Effortless inhibition: Habit mediates the relation between self-control and unhealthy snack consumption. *Frontiers in Psychology, 5,* 444.

4. Duhigg, Charles. (2012). *The power of habit: Why we do what we do in life and business*. Random House.

5. MIT researcher sheds light on why habits are hard to make and break. (1999, October 20). MIT News. Massachusetts Institute of Technology. https://news.mit.edu/1999/habits.

6. Brewer, J. (2019). Mindfulness training for addictions: Has neuroscience revealed a brain hack by which awareness subverts the addictive process? *Current Opinion in Psychology, 28,* 198–203.

7. Ludwig, V. U., Brown, K. W., & Brewer, J. A. (2020). Self-regulation without force: Can awareness leverage reward to drive behavior change? *Perspectives on Psychological Science, 15*(6), 1382–1399.

8. Hill, D. (2021, October 2). The Neuroscience of Habits. Psychology Today. https://www.psychologytoday.com/ca/blog/striving-thriving/202110/the-neuroscience-habits.

9. Hill, D. (n.d.). Use ACT to change unhelpful habits into values-rich habits. https://drdianahill.com/. https://drdianahill.com/resources/UseACTToChangeUnhelpfulHabitsintoValues-richHabits.pdf.

10. Clear, J. (2020, February 4). *Habit Stacking: How to Build New Habits by Taking Advantage of Old Ones*. James Clear. https://jamesclear.com/habit-stacking.

Chapter 27

1. World Health Organization: WHO. (2022b). Blood safety and availability. www.who.int. https://www.who.int/NEWS-ROOM/FACT-SHEETS/DETAIL/BLOOD-SAFETY-AND-AVAILABILITY.

2. Titmuss, R. (2018). *The gift relationship: From human blood to social policy*. Policy Press.

3. Ludwig, V. U., Brown, K. W., & Brewer, J. A. (2020). Self-regulation without force: Can awareness leverage reward to drive behavior change? *Perspectives on Psychological Science, 15*(6), 1382–1399.

4. Ryan, R. M., & Deci, E. L. (2017). *Self-determination theory: Basic psychological needs in motivation, development, and wellness*. New York: Guilford Press.

5. Aldao, A., Nolen-Hoeksema, S., & Schweizer, S. (2010). Emotion-regulation strategies across psychopathology: A meta-analytic review. *Clinical Psychology Review, 30*(2), 217–237.

6. Appleton, K. M., & McGowan, L. (2006). The relationship between restrained eating and poor psychological health is moderated by pleasure normally associated with eating. *Eating Behaviors, 7*(4), 342–347.

7. Friese, M., & Hofmann, W. (2016). State mindfulness, self-regulation, and emotional experience in everyday life. *Motivation Science, 2*(1), 1–14.

Chapter 28

1. 6 rituals and traditions from successful creative teams. Inside Design Blog. (n.d.). https://www.invisionapp.com/inside-design/6-rituals-and-traditions/.

2. Giovagnoli, R. (2017, June). From habits to rituals. In *Proceedings* (Vol. 1, No. 3, p. 225). MDPI.

3. Brooks, A. W., Schroeder, J., Risen, J. L., Gino, F., Galinsky, A. D., Norton, M. I., & Schweitzer, M. E. (2016). Don't stop believing: Rituals improve performance by decreasing anxiety. *Organizational Behavior and Human Decision Processes, 137*, 71–85.

4. Hobson, N. M., Schroeder, J., Risen, J. L., Xygalatas, D., & Inzlicht, M. (2018). The psychology of rituals: An integrative review and process-based framework. *Personality and Social Psychology Review, 22*(3), 260–284.

5. Norton, M. I., & Gino, F. (2014). Rituals alleviate grieving for loved ones, lovers, and lotteries. *Journal of Experimental Psychology: General, 143*(1), 266.

6. Rituals at work: Teams that play together stay together. (2022, March 24). HBS Working Knowledge. https://hbswk.hbs.edu/item/rituals-at-work-teams-that-play-together-stay-together.

7. Kim, T., Sezer, O., Schroeder, J., Risen, J., Gino, F., & Norton, M. I. (2021). Work group rituals enhance the meaning of work. *Organizational Behavior and Human Decision Processes, 165*, 197–212.

8. Tami, K. (2023, March 23). Personal communication [Personal interview].

9. Bloom, N., Liang, J., Roberts, J., & Ying, Z. J. (2015). Does working from home work? Evidence from a Chinese experiment. *The Quarterly Journal of Economics, 130*(1), 165–218; How working from home works out. (n.d.). Stanford Institute for

Economic Policy Research (SIEPR). https://siepr.stanford.edu/publications/policy-brief/how-working-home-works-out.

10. Bloom, N. (2023, March 6). Personal communication [Personal interview]; WFH Research. Survey of Working Arrangements and Attitudes. (n.d.). https://www.wfhresearch.com/.

11. Twaronite, K. (2019, March 21). The surprising power of simply asking coworkers how they're doing. *Harvard Business Review*. https://hbr.org/2019/02/the-surprising-power-of-simply-asking-coworkers-how-theyre-doing.

12. Team bonding: Exploring how mandatory and optional activities affect employees. Nulab. (n.d.). Nulab. https://nulab.com/learn/collaboration/team-bonding-exploring-how-mandatory-and-optional-activities-affect-employees/.

13. Kim, T., Sezer, O., Schroeder, J., Risen, J., Gino, F., & Norton, M. I. (2021). Work group rituals enhance the meaning of work. *Organizational Behavior and Human Decision Processes*, *165*, 197–212.

Chapter 29

1. Waldinger, R. (n.d.). What makes a good life? Lessons from the longest study on happiness [Video]. TED Talks. https://www.ted.com/talks/robert_waldinger_what_makes_a_good_life_lessons_from_the_longest_study_on_happiness/transcript?language=en.

2. Holt-Lunstad, J., Smith, T. B., & Layton, J. B. (2010). Social relationships and mortality risk: A meta-analytic review. *PLoS Medicine*, *7*(7), e1000316.

3. Eisenberger, N. I., & Cole, S. W. (2012). Social neuroscience and health: neurophysiological mechanisms linking social ties with physical health. *Nature Neuroscience*, *15*(5), 669–674.

4. Santini, Z. I., Koyanagi, A., Tyrovolas, S., Mason, C., & Haro, J. M. (2015). The association between social relationships and depression: A systematic review. *Journal of Affective Disorders*, *175*, 53–65.

5. Kuiper, J. S., Zuidersma, M., Voshaar, R. C. O., Zuidema, S. U., van den Heuvel, E. R., Stolk, R. P., & Smidt, N. (2015). Social relationships and risk of dementia: A systematic review and meta-analysis of longitudinal cohort studies. *Aging Research Reviews*, *22*, 39–57.

6. Eisenberger, N. I., Master, S. L., Inagaki, T. K., Taylor, S. E., Shirinyan, D., Lieberman, M. D., & Naliboff, B. D. (2011). Attachment figures

activate a safety signal-related neural region and reduce pain experience. *Proceedings of the National Academy of Sciences, 108*(28), 11721–11726.

7. Mineo, L. (2023, April 5). Over nearly 80 years, Harvard study has been showing how to live a healthy and happy life. *Harvard Gazette.* https://news.harvard.edu/gazette/story/2017/04/over-nearly-80-years-harvard-study-has-been-showing-how-to-live-a-healthy-and-happy-life/.

8. Ruggles, S. (2007). The decline of intergenerational coresidence in the United States, 1850 to 2000. *American Sociological Review, 72*(6), 964–989.

9. Fry, R., Passel, J. S., & Cohn, D. (2020, September 9). A majority of young adults in the U.S. live with their parents for the first time since the Great Depression. Pew Research Center. https://www.pewresearch.org/fact-tank/2020/09/04/a-majority-of-young-adults-in-the-u-s-live-with-their-parents-for-the-first-time-since-the-great-depression/.

10. Treleaven, S. (2021). Platonic parenting: Why more people are having babies with friends—*Today's Parent.* https://www.todaysparent.com/family/parenting/platonic-parenting-having-babies-with-friends/.

11. The Teen Brain: 7 Things to Know. (n.d.). National Institute of Mental Health (NIMH). https://www.nimh.nih.gov/health/publications/the-teen-brain-7-things-to-know.

12. Neill, A. S. (1962). *Summerhill.* Pocket Books, 4.

13. CBS News. (2006, November 19). No grades, no tests at "Free School." CBS News. https://www.cbsnews.com/news/no-grades-no-tests-at-free-school/.

14. Press—Brooklyn Free School. (n.d.). Brooklyn Free School. https://www.brooklynfreeschool.org/press.

15. Carney, B. (2018, November 4). Give your team the freedom to do the work they think matters most. *Harvard Business Review.* https://hbr.org/2018/09/give-your-team-the-freedom-to-do-the-work-they-think-matters-most.

16. See note 15.

17. Palmarès Best Workplaces France 2018. Great Place to Work France. (n.d.). https://www.greatplacetowork.fr/palmares/tous-nos-palmares/palmares-2018/.

Index